Power Pl

Five Plays to Read
Perform

Paul Francis

Edward Arnold

© Paul Francis 1981

First published 1981 by
Edward Arnold (Publishers) Ltd
41 Bedford Square
London WC1B 3DQ

British Library Cataloguing in Publication Data

Francis, Paul
    Power plays.
    I. Title
    822'.9'14

ISBN 0-7131-0514-3

The Author wishes to acknowledge the following source
material:
The Untouchables: Eliot Ness with Oscar Fraley (Hodder &
Stoughton 1967)
Al Capone: F. D. Pasley (Faber Paperbacks 1966)
A Textile Community in the Industrial Revolution: E. G. Power
(Longman 1969)

Phototypeset in Linotron 202 Palatino by
Western Printing Services Ltd, Bristol
Printed in Great Britain by
Spottiswoode Ballantyne Ltd, Colchester and London

Contents

Introduction

The plays in this collection were not written as a series, although they do have themes in common. Their language is not difficult, but I have tried to tackle situations and ideas that are worthy of adult interest. Our past history and the recurrent problems of power justify classroom attention and are also accessible to most pupils in secondary schools. There is, too, a value in connecting the individual study of character and the social study of contexts, rather than confining them to separate disciplines. A common concern thus runs through all five plays, but they vary considerably in length, mood and style of staging, and the unwary should be warned against simply working through them one at a time.

The plays are intended for classroom reading, dramatic performance and individual study. As an aid to study I have included some of my own teaching ideas at the back of the book, but as usual these can be adapted, amplified or ignored. They should certainly not be presented as an invariable diet for all consumers. The plays should generate discussion as well as written work, and teachers will need to decide for themselves about priorities and teaching approaches.

The plays are also intended as a spur to dramatic writing, by both staff and pupils. There are obvious advantages in producing a home-grown text for performance: length, balance of parts and areas of difficulty can all be more carefully controlled, and special needs can be more easily met.

Less familiar, perhaps, is the setting of play-writing tasks to pupils. The structural demands of the two-hour play may well be beyond most teenagers, but all pupils can attempt the writing of dialogue. Concentration on direct speech will rescue some pupils from the problems of sustained writing in prose, and also encourages the simultaneous awareness of different points of view which is a vital stage in the process of maturity. There can also be a real enjoyment in learning the craft of play building, of shaping scenes, contrasting moods and constructing climaxes. By providing accessible models this collection should help pupils to develop a more sophisticated sense of dramatic technique in action – and that should lead to more enjoyment in performance, writing and appreciation.

P.F.

A Whole Lot of Grief

There's a lot of grief in this limelight.
Al Capone

Al Capone	**Eliot Ness**
Lombardo	**Howard**
Fred	**Dave**
Joe	**Basile, Ness' driver**
Hymie	**Lawyer**
The Kid	**Newsboy**
Tony the Greek	**Mrs. Freeman**
O'Banion, *gangster and*	**Policeman**
florist	**Widow**
Chief of Police	**Drunk**
Detective-Sergeant	**Narrator**

The play takes place in Chicago, in the 1920s.

A Note on Staging:
Scene One presents a series of comments, direct to the audience, from isolated figures spread across the stage. After Scene Two, the settings of the play alternate between the gangster and police worlds, probably set on opposite sides of the stage. In any case, very little furniture is needed, and movement from scene to scene should be as smooth as possible.

Scene One

Song All you want can be yours for a bullet,
So write out your claim and your will,
The small guy can end up a big shot
Provided he's ready to kill;
There's a whole lot of grief in the limelight
When you're climbing up there on your own,
Keep your mind and your hand on the trigger
And who cares what a harvest you've sown?

1

Narrator:	Chicago, in the 1920s. Alcohol is illegal – which means it costs a little more. The extra money, and anything else worth having, goes to Al Capone. He controls beer, business and the police. He's a lot of different things to a lot of different people.
Lawyer:	Capone makes justice impossible. In four years there have been 135 gang killings, only six of which have come to trial. The only man to be sentenced committed murder in a courtroom.
Newsboy:	I was on my corner, still had fifty papers to sell and it was raining. Like stairrods, it was. I was soaked. Then this guy comes up and asks me how many I've got left, and I tell him. He gives me twenty dollars, tells me to get out of the rain. Then he picks up his papers and dumps them in the gutter. That was Mister Capone.
Mrs. Freeman:	We were shopping in town when the O'Banion gang tried to kill Capone in a cafe. They fired a thousand shots in ten seconds and our car was caught in the middle. I had to have six operations try to save the sight of one eye. Mr. Capone paid for all of them: ten thousand dollars' worth.
Policeman:	I'm a Chicago cop. If you're not in it, you don't understand. It looks bad, taking extra money, not arresting guys you know have done something. But it ain't that bad. Everybody gets their cut and it's all organised. And the guys that get killed are crooks, mostly.
Widow:	My husband was a policeman. He found one of the Capone gang wrongly parked and asked for his licence – they just shot him in the face. He never had a chance.
Drunk:	Way, I see it, Mishter Capone – hic! – is jesht a public servant Sheems the government don't like no drinkin, but I likesh it fine . . . hic! . . .
Citizen:	We don't vote, we don't do jury duty, we don't go around too much at night, or round the Loop at any time. It isn't that we like the way things are; we just happen to be scared of dying.
Narrator:	And in Chicago, in the twenties, most people have something to fear . . .

Scene Two

Tony the Greek's cafe, deserted. Tony whistles happily, polishing tables. Al Capone enters, suspiciously.

Tony: Al, Good to see you. (*Al looks round*) Come on, Al, you're safe here.

Al: Maybe, maybe. (*He sits down, facing the door.*) That's better.

Tony: Bit tense tonight, eh?

Al: Mm?

Tony: You're a bit nervy tonight, aren't you?

Al: (*turning angrily*): Who's nervy?

Tony: Well, I mean . . .

Al: You saying I'm chicken, huh?

Tony: Now Al, come on. I feed you, don't I? Always, I feed you . . .

Al: Yeh, you do. Sorry, Tony, I guess I am a bit edgy.

Tony: Just you relax, and I'll fix your favourite spaghetti. What is it, the cops?

Al: Cops? You're joking. Those guys – I got them just here (*puts thumb down on the table*). You want an arrest, you don't want an arrest – you see me. I tell the cops what they do.

Tony: Then what's wrong?

Al: Ah, the whole racket.

Tony: You're not going straight?

Al: Tony, don't make me laugh. Now what would I do a dumb thing like that for? I wouldn't know how to start. I put too much into this to give up now. Remember me at the beginning, Tony?

Tony: I should do, Al. You got my best spaghetti, then, for nothing. For nothing.

Al: Not bad, eh, for Johnny Torrio's little lad. Give Al the trouble, they said, he'll handle it. Not bad, eh? That's what they said. And now I make the trouble. Pretty good, huh?

Tony: Yeh, you come a long way since those days. And you always come back to Tony for your spaghetti.

Al: That's it, Tony. You gotta have places to come. You can be king or nothing but you've gotta have somewhere to go, somewhere you're known, where you're safe.

Tony: So who's after you, Al?

Al: Just about everyone – bar the cops. The Irish, O'Banion, all the guys I've taken over – even my own people.

Tony: It's a tough game.

Al: It's not a game, Tony, it's a war. Once you're in, you're in, and they never let you go. You keep talking and killing, 'cos the day you go soft you lose, and you can't afford to lose, not that way.

Tony: But you're doing all right?

Al   *(not wholly convincing)*: Oh, I'm fine, just fine. Expanding all the time. *(The kitchen bell rings, Tony goes to the hatch to fetch the spaghetti and returns with it. He puts it in front of Al.)*

Tony: There you are, Al. Your spaghetti. You won't get that round the corner, and you know it's OK, huh? *(He slaps Al's back cheerfully. Capone stiffens, and looks at him.)* What's the matter?

Al: They tried to get me. My own chef. Ten thousand dollars to put prussic acid in my soup.

Tony: Now, Al, that's not true.

Al: He told me. Ten thousand dollars. For twenty I reckon he'd have done it.

Tony: But you can trust me, Al.

Al: I can trust you, Tony, but how many more?

Tony: Come on, eat your spaghetti.

Al: One day, they'll get the twenty thousand and that'll be it. Capone – R.I.P.

Tony: But you're big, Al, very big. Your men, they look after you.

Al   *(as if Tony has not spoken)*: Watching. All the time you're watching. You have to, 'cos the minute you let up – that's it.

Tony: Well, you're OK here. Come on, Al, eat.

Al: You're right, Tony. I'm sorry. *(Al starts to eat, slowly. The kitchen bell goes, and he stops. His hand goes to his pocket.)* What's that?

Tony: Relax, Al. My kitchen. *(Goes to phone.)* Yes?

Al   *(anxious)*: Everything OK?

Tony: Sure it's OK. *(To the phone)* Enrico? Now whassamatter, huh? Me and Mister Capone we're talking, OK? . . . You what? Oh, you are babies, the lot of you. Babies . . . Yes, all right, I am coming. Look out. *(Slams down phone.)*

Al: What's up?

Tony: Don't worry. My kitchen staff, they are crazy, I swear it. One minute, Al, I sort them out. One minute only. You eat. *(Tony goes out, leaving Al sitting. He toys with his meal, but can't start. After an anxious silence, a muffled shot. Al goes to the phone and rings.)*

Al: Hello, hello . . . Tony? Tony, what's happening . . . Tony? *(He puts it down slowly and sits down.)* Oh, Tony, not you, why do they get you? *(He sits at the table, his head in his hands.)*

Scene Three

O'Banion's flower shop. O'Banion, a gangster who also runs a flower shop, is stylishly dressed. He is busy arranging flowers with his back to the door as the Kid enters, eager and awkward. O'Banion swivels and draws his gun.

Kid:	Mister Banion? (*Sees the gun.*) What's the matter, aren't you one of Mister Capone's friends any more?
O'Banion:	I don't think I'm anyone's friend.
Kid:	But I thought –
O'Banion:	And if it comes to that I don't think he's got any friends either.
Kid:	But he's one of your top customers.
O'Banion:	So what? He kills people, he sends 'em flowers . . . and I'm a florist. That's not friendship.
Kid	(*reaching to an inside pocket*): But I've got a –
O'Banion:	Stop. Keep your hands where I can see them. You new to this?
Kid:	Well, I . . . er . . . I guess.
O'Banion:	Nothing to be ashamed of. Just a fact.
Kid:	So?
O'Banion:	So, learn something without being killed. How many guns I got?
Kid:	I dunno. Two?
O'Banion:	I'll tell you. Three. (*He pats his pockets in turn.*) There, . . . there . . . and here. And if I'd only had two I'd have died two summers ago.
Kid:	Gee, I'm sorry, Mister Banion.
O'Banion:	The name is *O*'Banion, and you don't have to be sorry – just careful. Now, what you got for me? (*Kid reaches towards pocket with right hand.*) No, left hand. (*Kid slowly picks out the note with his left hand, and hands it over.*)
Kid:	A note from Mister Capone.
O'Banion:	What does Scarface want now, more wreaths?
Kid:	I don't know.
O'Banion:	Yeah, that's it; listen to this – 'Dear Dion, I shall require the usual merchandise tomorrow at three o'clock prompt. Three of my officials will come straight from business to collect same. Please oblige.' That guy slays me. He didn't write like that when he started. Still, a lot of things have changed.
Kid:	Did you know Mister Capone, then, at the beginning?
O'Banion:	Kid, I was a big man around here when Scarface was running messages for Johnny Torrio.

Kid:	Gee, that's terrific.
O'Banion:	Not really, it just happens. Still, keep to now. Who's the merchandise for, then?
Kid:	I don't get you.
O'Banion:	Kid, don't be dumber than you have to. Al doesn't order a thousand dollar wreath just for the flowers. Who's getting it?
Kid:	I dunno. Honest, Mister Banion, he just said to take the message.
O'Banion	(*wearily*): O'Banion. OK, Kid, you're dumb but straight – straight as anyone, that is. Drop in for your wreath tomorrow, it'll be ready. You on the chopper?
Kid:	Er . . . I . . .
O'Banion:	Are you doing the job, rubbing out, torpedo?
Kid:	Oh, er, yes . . . I guess.
O'Banion:	First time, eh? (*Kid is silent.*) Don't worry, you'll get used to it. It's amazing what you can get used to.
Kid:	Cheerio, Mister Ban – Mister O'Banion. (*He hurries to leave. O'Banion watches him, and shakes his head. He goes back to his flowers.*)

Scene Four

The office of the Chief of Police. Eliot Ness and his driver Basile are sitting outside, waiting. The Detective Sergeant comes out of the office, and nods for Ness to go in.

Ness:	Wish me luck, Basile.
Basile:	If you're sure you want it.
Ness:	I want it. (*He goes into the office.*)
Basile:	God help you, I think you really do. (*Basile remains seated, waiting as the action moves to inside the office.*)
Chief:	Well, Ness, I can give you five minutes.
Ness:	I want to talk about Capone, sir.
Chief:	You've still only got five minutes.
Ness:	Sir, at the moment we can't move. Ninety per cent of crime in Chicago is run by Capone and on the other ten per cent we can't do a thing because everyone knows he's got the force sewn up.
Detective-Sergeant:	We know that.
Ness:	You know it!
Chief:	Of course we know it. We're not stupid. What do you expect us to do?

Ness:	Arrest him.
Chief:	On what charge? What witnesses? There's no one in this town who'll swear to seeing Capone go through a red light, let alone kill anyone.
Detective-Sergeant:	And these days he gets all his killing done for him.
Chief	(*leafing through papers, as though Ness has finished*): Is that all you wanted, Ness?
Ness:	No, sir. I . . . I want to make a suggestion.
Chief:	About Capone?
Ness:	Yes, sir.
Chief:	Go on.
Ness:	I think we ought to go after him. He's the key to everything that happens. We can't work while he's loose.
Chief:	So?
Ness:	If we can't arrest him now we ought to work till we can. Have a small group, really good, absolutely watertight, working till they get evidence. (*Chief scribbles, appearing to lose interest.*)
Detective-Sergeant:	And where do we get these men from?
Ness:	Pick 'em. Go through the records, again and again. Look for straight, tough detectives, good and hard. You want a dozen cops Capone's never touched and never will.
Detective-Sergeant:	And even if you find them, what then?
Ness:	Take them out of the main force, to work on their own. It's a full-time Capone squad. They mustn't be in with the force as a whole.
Detective-Sergeant:	And what do they do?
Ness:	Collect evidence, close down his breweries, hold his beer trucks – anything that'll weaken him.
Detective-Sergeant:	You think we can get a dozen men who can do that?
Ness:	If there aren't twelve straight cops in the whole of Chicago we've had it anyway.
Detective-Sergeant	(*after some thought*): Perhaps you're right.
Ness:	So you agree?
Chief:	Ness, you've nearly had your five minutes.
Ness:	I know, sir, but –
Chief:	And there is one other thing.
Ness:	Sir?
Chief:	These dozen men. How do they stay alive?
Ness:	Capone kills other gangsters. He doesn't kill cops.
Chief:	He doesn't kill cops because he doesn't need to. Not at the moment, anyway. And the gangsters he kills are the ones who get in his way. I take it that the squad you're suggesting might also get in Capone's way?
Ness:	Oh yes, we'd break him.

Chief:	We?
Ness:	I'm sorry, sir, but if this squad is formed, I'd . . . I'd very much like to be in it.
Chief:	I'm afraid I can't promise that.
Ness:	Oh.
Chief:	You see, I can't tell you anything about the squad. Because if it's going to work it'll have to be completely independent – even I can't decide who's in it or how it works. The leader will pick his team and do what he needs to as long as he gets Capone. That's the risk I have to take.
Ness:	I see.
Chief:	So it's up to you. (*He returns his papers, as if bored. Slowly, Ness realises what he's said.*)
Ness:	Up to me? You mean . . . oh, thank you, sir.
Chief	(*without looking up*): Thank you, Ness, your five minutes are up. **(Detective-Sergeant escorts Ness to the door, and then returns. Ness rushes to Basile, who is reading a paper.)**
Ness:	I made it, Basile, I made it. We've got the job.
Basile:	Congratulations – but I think you're out of your head.

Scene Five

O'Banion's flower shop, as before. O'Banion is finishing a huge wreath. Fred and Lombardo enter silently, with the Kid. They push him forward.

Kid:	Mister O'Banion?
	(*As before, O'Banion swivels and draws. As he sees the Kid he puts his gun back, but still watches the other two.*)
Fred:	What a reflex. I thought you were expecting us.
Lombardo:	Not a very friendly reception.
O'Banion	(*still tense*): I'm sorry, I didn't –
Lombardo:	That's all right. (*Walking forward*) It's a pleasure to do business with a real professional.
Fred:	It is that. A real privilege.
	(Fred walks forward with his right hand outstretched. As O'Banion shakes it, the Kid grabs his left arm and Lombardo shoots him in the back. It is all very quick and skilful.)
Lombardo:	OK, Fred, that'll do. Out. Well done, Kid, now move.
Kid	(*dazed*): You mean just leave him?
Lombardo:	What d'you want to do, hold a funeral?

Fred	(*picks up the wreath, and throws it onto O'Banion's feet*): He's got his flowers already. Let's go. (*He goes out.*)
Lombardo:	Come on, kid, you did your bit. You're OK.
Kid:	But . . . I killed him . . .
Lombardo:	Yeah, so did I, and Fred, and Scarface – but we're all alive. That's how it works.
Kid:	But it's . . . oh, hell.
Lombardo:	Sure it is. But we didn't make it that way. Besides, we got him before he got us. Didn't you hear his men got Tony the Greek? (*He goes to the door.*) Come on, the cops won't wait for ever. (*The Kid looks at him, then at O'Banion's body, and then follows Lombardo out.*)
Song	You just can't afford to have rivals, If you can't reach a man get his friend But beware of the smile and the handshake And the flowers your enemies send: There's a whole lot of grief in the limelight When you're standing up there on your own, Keep your mind and your hand on the trigger And who cares if your heart turns to stone?

Scene Six

The office of Eliot Ness' special Capone squad. Howard is busy working on figures as Ness enters.

Ness:	How do we stand, Howard?
Howard:	I can't get the full estimate, but I think we're beginning to hurt.
Ness:	Go on.
Howard:	Well, the depot you smashed into last week cost him fifty thousand direct. That should cut his income for a bit, but then there's . . .
Dave	(*entering cheerfully*): Happy Valentine, crime fighters. How many cards d'you get, Howard?
Howard:	I lost count.
Dave:	Tt tt, and you in charge of records, too.
Ness:	Dave, we've got to work, so if it's not urgent –
Dave:	Oh, but it is, it is. Unless, that is, you're too busy to hear about the murder of seven O'Banion men. Seven little gangsters, bullets in the head.

9

Ness:	All right, what happened?
Dave:	Well, you know O'Banion's men were sore about their boss getting hit at the flower store?
Howard:	Well?
Dave:	Well, it seems they tried to get Scarface. Put a thousand bullets into his pet cafe. Well, today they get told.
Ness:	How?
Dave:	Capone sent three men disguised as cops into the Clark Street garage. They lined the O'Banions up against the wall to search them, just a routine check. So the O'Banions line up, face the wall, and then all of a sudden there's a man with a machine gun and we're seven villains less.
Howard:	Phew!
Dave:	You've got to admit, it's a very neat job.
Howard:	That's murder, impersonating a police officer . . .
Ness:	Hold it, Howard.
Howard:	What's the problem?
Ness:	Witnesses?
Howard	(*to Dave*): Well, where d'you get the story from?
Dave:	Very special friends. They're nearly too scared to breathe as it is. Make a case of it and they'll testify in coffins.
Howard:	And they got all seven dead, just like that?
Dave:	Well, not quite. Frank Gusenberg was still alive when we got to him.
Howard:	What did he say?
Dave:	'Nobody shot me' – that's all he said 'Nobody shot me.'
Howard:	What a fool. Protecting his enemy.
Ness:	No, Howard, for them there's only one real enemy, and that's us. They fight over territory, beat each other up now and again and kill when they're really mad, but we're the people they hate.
Howard:	And what are we going to do?
Ness:	Just keep going. Get hold of Capone's agents, close down his breweries, cut down his profits and pray that he cracks before we do.
Dave:	I hope you're right, chief.
Howard:	Eliot?
Ness:	Mmm?
Howard:	Even if you're right, even if Capone does crack, what is he actually going to do? When a guy like Capone cracks, what happens?
Ness:	I don't know. I just want to find out.
Howard:	It could be bad.

Dave:	He's right, chief. Someone's going to get hurt.
Ness	(*suddenly angry*): And you think I don't know that? Drive a man like Capone to the end of his tether and hundreds of people get hurt. But look at it now, the whole of Chicago gets hurt. D'you want that?
Dave:	I don't, but a lot of guys seem to.
Ness:	A lot of guys seem to want a kick in the seat, and we might make sure they get it. We'll just have to be very careful.

Scene Seven

Al Capone's headquarters, in an expensive hotel room. Fred, Joe and the Kid are talking, as Lombardo watches the door.

Lombardo:	Hey, you guys, shut up. (*As Al enters, they stop talking.*)
Al:	Right, who's this Ness?
Joe:	He's a cop.
Al	(*very sarcastic*): Really? You don't say? He's arresting every liquor agent I got and he's actually a cop? Now, who'd have guessed that? Dumb, the lot of you. Why haven't we got him?
Lombardo:	He can't be got, boss.
Al:	What d'you mean, can't?
Lombardo:	He don't want money.
Joe:	Hey, a cop who don't want money, how about . . . (*He stops as Al glares at him.*)
Al	(*to Lombardo*): Scare him then.
Lombardo:	We tried it, Al. Least, Eddie tried it. He's still in hospital, with an attempted murder rap waiting when he gets better.
Al:	This Ness, he's got a wife, hasn't he?
Lombardo:	They're awful close, boss. We're working on it.
Al:	Working on it! I'm losing a steady three thousand a week and a helluva lot of equipment and you're working on it.
Fred:	It isn't that easy, Mister Capone –
Joe:	You see –
Al:	See! All I see is me losing profit and I wanna know why. I'm big round here, aren't I?
Joe:	Sure.
Al:	And what I say goes, right?
Joe:	Sure, Al. I mean, Mister Capone.

Al:	Right. Well, what I say right now is that Ness is in my hair and I want him out. OK?
Lombardo:	Sure, boss, but –
Al:	I don't want the buts. Is that OK?
Fred:	We get it.
Al:	That's fine. You get it. All you have to do is do it. By Thursday. (*He goes out, angry.*)
Lombardo:	Thursday!
Fred:	Relax, it's only Tuesday night.
Lombardo:	What d'you mean, *only*?
Joe:	Well, there's four of us, and this Ness can't be that good.
Lombardo:	Listen, bonehead. Have you actually seen Ness?
Fred:	Well, I've heard plenty but I ain't actually seen him.
Lombardo:	Well, I have and he is big, and mean, and very, very quick.
Joe:	We know that, but –
Lombardo:	I'm not kidding. If I had to go after one man I'd rather go for Scarface than Ness.
Joe:	You what?
Lombardo:	Don't get me wrong. I work for Al, fine. But I'm not going after Ness.
Fred:	His wife?
Lombardo:	Too close.
Fred:	Anyone else?
Joe:	There's a driver.
Fred:	What?
Joe:	Guy called Basile. Big buddies for a long time. He lives pretty near, but not too near. 52nd street, corner of 43rd. Drives Ness everywhere, and he doesn't carry a gun.
Fred:	Well, that's OK then.
Lombardo:	You wouldn't like to mention it before?
Joe:	Sorry, Lombardo, I guess I forgot.
Lombardo:	Forgot! You nearly had Al on our backs for weeks. Well, drop it for now. 52nd street, corner of 43rd. OK?
Fred:	When?
Lombardo:	Tomorrow. 2.30. Right? Fred, you pick up Hymie.
Fred:	Is that Hymie Weiss?
Lombardo:	That's right. Anything wrong?
Fred:	Nothing. Nothing at all.
Lombardo:	That's all right, then. OK, Kid?
Kid:	Yeh. Yeh, sure.
Lombardo:	Right. Be there. (*He goes out.*)

Scene Eight

Eliot Ness' office. Ness is sitting, silent and thoughtful, when Howard comes in, very energetic.

Howard: Eliot, I've got those figures on the breweries.

Ness: Yeah? Oh, well . . .

Howard: Eliot, we've got a breakthrough. We really are getting somewhere. I'm telling you, we – what's the matter?

Ness: Capone. He . . .

Howard: Look, chief, if you're not interested . . .

Ness: Of course I'm interested. I'm not chasing this guy twenty-four hours a day just for laughs, am I?

Howard: I guess not. So what's up?

Ness: They got Basile.

Howard: What?

Ness: My driver Basile. They got him.

Howard: I'm sorry, chief.

Ness: It just means we're going to have to be that bit better, that's all. (*Dave enters frantically.*)

Dave: Eliot, Eliot, they've got Basile.

Ness: I know.

Dave: The only guy we have who doesn't shoot, and they have to get him.

Ness: That's why they got him.

Howard: You seem very calm.

Ness: I'm not calm. Don't think that. But Scarface wants me mad. He wants me wild, so I'll do something crazy. So just for him, I'll stay cool. But I'm not calm. I just want Capone.

Dave: You're not going in, chief?

Ness: What with, a peashooter?

Dave: Just an idea.

Ness: Well, forget it. That hotel is crawling. If you got a mouse in it would be half lead by the time it reached the landing.

Howard: And where is Capone?

Ness: Sitting in state, on the fifth floor, watching the traffic run through his kingdom . . . which might be an idea. (*Ness grows more decisive, as Dave and Howard watch, baffled.*)

Dave: What is it?

Ness: A gesture from Basile to Scarface. How many drivers have we got at the station, Dave?

Dave: 'Bout twenty.

Ness: Get them all, now. And about twenty-five more. I want forty-five drivers, and I don't care where they're from.

Howard:	Are you giving Basile a gangster funeral or something?
Ness:	Not quite. (*He doodles, calmly, on a piece of paper.*)
Dave:	What are you going to do, then, just sit on your backside?
Howard:	I suppose you've got a better idea?
Ness:	That's right, Dave, I'm going to sit on my backside. And I'm going to see a few people, and then I'm going to ring Capone.
Dave:	Eliot, whatever for?
Ness:	To tell him what's going to happen.
Dave:	And what is going to happen?
Ness:	That's a little secret for Al and me. I'll see you. (*Goes out.*)
Howard:	It's finally happened. He's crazy.
Dave:	Yeah, but he does get results. He's worrying Capone.
Howard:	Dead right. It's all there, and it's thanks to Eliot. But this, just now. He has a close friend shot and he decides he's not going to do anything but ring Capone. I don't get it.
Dave:	It'll be all right.
Howard:	How d'you mean?
Dave:	Eliot looks as though he knows what's going to happen. And if he knows it and likes it, you can bet your life Capone won't.
Howard:	I hope you're right. (*He goes on with paper work, as Dave goes out.*)

Scene Nine

Capone's headquarters, with Lombardo alone, pacing uneasily. Fred, Joe and Hymie enter, looking confident.

Lombardo:	Well?
Hymie:	Hi, Lombardo. Whaddya mean, well?
Joe:	Easy as that.
Fred:	Huh. Such a big shot.
Lombardo:	You did get Basile?
Joe:	It was like taking sweets from a kid.
Lombardo:	It should be. He didn't carry a gun.
Hymie:	That Ness'll have to find himself a new driver.
Joe:	And there won't be many going for that job, hey?
Fred:	How's Al, then?
Lombardo:	Not good. Where's the kid?

Fred:	He got his, hung around waiting for the cops. Like at O'Banions. Only this time they came.
Lombardo:	He won't talk?
Fred:	Not a word. He was soft, anyway. Only a kid.
	(*Al Capone enters, worried.*)
Al:	You get him, that Basile?
Fred:	We got him.
Joe:	Ness knows he'll be next, boss. You won't hear from him.
Al:	I just have.
Joe:	You what?
Al:	I just have. Ness just rang me.
Joe:	What did he say – can I have my driver back? (*Laughs, briefly.*)
Lombardo:	Close it.
Fred:	What did Ness want?
Al:	I don't know. I can't work it out.
Lombardo:	Well, what did he say?
Al:	You did get Basile, didn't you?
Hymie:	Sure we got him. That's what you paid for, that's what you got.
Fred:	I checked.
Al:	And Ness knows we got him?
Fred:	Must do by now.
Lombardo:	What's up, then, Al?
Al:	Ness. He rang me. He didn't sound bothered. Very cool. He said to say there was a good show on, and to watch the window.
Joe	(*grabbing gun*): It's a trick, boss. (*He moves to the window.*)
Lombardo:	We know it's a trick, Joey, that's the point. But what sort of trick? Why does he want you here, boss?
Al:	I don't know, do I?
Hymie:	Don't you worry, Mister Capone. I'll take care of the cop.
Fred:	Maybe.
Joe:	Gee, boss, he wouldn't get past the doorman. 'N if he did, he'd go out with a wooden overcoat.
Al:	I know that, dumbbell. And what's more, Ness knows it. If a bonehead like you can work it out I reckon he might manage it. Lombardo, we got all our guards, ain't we?
Lombardo:	Yeah, I just checked.
Al:	Then what can he do?
Lombardo:	Search me.
Al:	Ah, you're no good to me. There's cops closing in on me, breaking up my world, and all you do is stand there. Why does Ness want me here?

Joe:	Well how the hell are we supposed to –
Al	(*very cold*): Yes?
Joe:	Oh . . . er . . . nothing. (*Hymie, at the window, beckons to Joe, who joins him.*)
Fred:	Could just be a stall, to get us thinking.
Lombardo:	He's done that, all right.
Hymie	(*looking out of the window*): Get a load of that.
Joe:	Hey, Lombardo, come here. (*Lombardo goes, as Al watches, suspiciously.*)
Al:	Are you guys holding out on me? What's going on?
Lombardo:	Some kind of parade, boss. They're clearing the street. Hey, it ain't a parade. It's the beer trucks, the ones Ness got.
Fred:	How many?
Lombardo:	Dunno. Six, seven . . . no, they're still coming.
Fred:	But what are they doing? Are they shooting?
Lombardo:	No. No, they're just going past the hotel, looking up. Dead slow, all of them. And they're still coming.
Hymie:	Hey, jus' look at them. All those trucks.
Al:	My trucks. He's stolen my trucks. That lousy copper's stolen my trucks. (*He turns to them*) Why didn't you kill him? . . . Well? (*Pause.*)
Hymie	(*quietly, to Joe*): That's thirty already, and they're not finished.
Al	(*menacing*): What are you crowing about?
Lombardo:	Every truck we ever owned.
Al:	We? Whaddya mean, we? Those are mine. He's riding my trucks in front of my hotel – and my men are just watching and cheering.
Lombardo:	We ain't cheering, boss.
Joe:	What d'you want us to do?
Al:	I want you to button your lip before you get taken for a ride.
Lombardo:	Al, we can't stop forty trucks.
Al:	Well, at least get away from that window. (*Uncertainly, they back away, but still look out from time to time. Al walks slowly to the window, and watches for a moment in silence.*) All right, Ness, very clever. You don't do that to me, nobody does that to me. Nobody, see (*Turns round, accusingly.*)
Hymie:	Sure, Mister Capone.
Al:	I fought for this territory. I got it from O'Banion and no fool cop is going to ride my trucks about town, understand? You guys get this – Ness or me is going to break, and Al Capone doesn't break. Not ever.
Lombardo:	That's right, boss.
Al:	I'm big and I aim to stay big, right?

Joe: Sure, boss, you said it.

Al: I want Ness dead. I want my trucks back and I want . . . I'm going to stay big and . . . and . . . get out, will ya. (*They stand, uncertain.*) Get out, I said. Will you guys get the hell out? Now! (*Almost a scream. They go, quickly and quietly. Al walks to the window, watches for a moment, and then sits, his head in his hands. The lights dim, but he stays seated, head in hands, until the end of the play.*)

Scene Ten

Narrator: One of them had to crack, and Ness stayed alive. Capone's power faded. After ten years of running Chicago, making sixty million dollars a year from liquor and ordering countless murders, the greatest gangster of all time was finally caught – for not paying his taxes. He was sentenced to a fine of fifty thousand dollars and eleven years in prison. In an interview before he was caught, this is what he said. (*Narrator turns on tape recorder, as Capone remains motionless.*)

Capone's Voice (*on tape*): During the last two years I've been trying to get out, but once in the racket you're always in . . . You fear death every moment. I never was able to leave my home without a bodyguard.

I haven't had peace of mind in years. I never know when I'm going to get it. Even when I'm on a peace errand I take a chance on the light suddenly going out . . . I have a wife and a boy I idolize at Palm Island, Florida. If I could go there and forget it all I would be the happiest man in the world. I want peace, and I'm willing to live and let live.

Narrator: His sentence was shortened to eight years for excellent conduct. Capone retired to Florida, where an early illness increasingly attacked his brain. He died, raving but in his bed, at the age of forty-eight.

Song You're so big that it's you that they're after,
Get a bullet-proof place you can hide,
You can hold up the world for a million
But it's life that takes you for a ride:
There's a whole lot of grief in the limelight
When you're dying up there on your own,
Lose your mind but your hand's on the trigger
And who cares if you're mad and alone?

Assassination

Marianne Heller, *a student and daughter of the Premier*
Petra, *her friend*
Marc, *Marianne's boyfriend*
Molluk, *Chief of Police*
Nilson, *a police officer*
Korpov, *a police officer*
Radio Announcer

Erik Heller, *Premier*
Mrs. Heller, *his wife*
The Student Committee:
Alex (*Chairman*)
Carlo
Andrei
Jerome
Kristina
Tomas, *a messenger*
Viktor

The play takes place in Durium, an imaginary European country. The time is the present.

Scene One

Marc, Marianne and Petra sit reading while the radio plays a current record. Marc is sprawled over a chair, while Petra is obviously studying. After a few moments, the record is interrupted by a radio announcement.

Radio Announcer:	We interrupt Pop Through Europe, and the current hit from England, to bring you an urgent announcement. The Premier, Mr. Erik Heller, will speak to the nation tonight about the student riots, and the measures the government will take.
Marc	(*switching the radio off*): There you are. Dad strikes again.
Marianne:	Oh shut up.
Marc:	He'll cut your grant for a start, reading when he's on the news.
Marianne	(*still reading*): Very funny.
Petra:	It's not Marianne's fault her dad's Premier.

Marianne:	Don't worry, Petra, it's Marc's idea of a joke.
Marc:	I don't see why I have to treat Heller with kid gloves just because he's Marianne's dad. If he's in the government, that makes him public property.
Petra:	If he's in the government the chances are he's got four times as much sense as you'll ever have. You could show a bit of respect.
Marc:	Oh yes. Obey the rulers, show respect and it'll all end up all right. Big Brother knows best.
Marianne:	All right, Marc. You know neither of you will change your minds, so why bother?
Marc:	I can't give up just because she won't listen. You don't get anywhere in politics if you give up as soon as you meet opposition.
Petra:	So I'm politics, am I? Thanks very much.
Marianne	(*to Marc*): You sound just like Dad. I think you're jealous.
Marc:	Jealous, of him?
Petra:	Why not? I bet you fancy yourself as Premier, don't you? Running everything your way and making the occasional speech to the nation.
Marianne:	That I can't wait to see.
Marc:	Well, I'll tell you one thing. If I ever did get to power at least I'd hang on to my beliefs.
Petra:	Meaning?
Marc:	Meaning I wouldn't get elected telling everyone I wanted freedom and then start filling up the jails in six months.
Petra:	What are you on about?
Marianne:	Marc thinks my dad ought to open up all the jails because he believes in free speech.
Petra:	But the only people he's locked up are communists.
Marc:	How do you know?
Petra:	He said so, on the last broadcast.
Marc:	If the radio said the earth was flat you'd believe it. I know one of the blokes he's interned, and he left the communists last year.
Petra:	That's what he says. I'd rather he was locked up.
Marc:	Yeah, and for how long?
Petra:	I don't know. Till the situation calms down.
Marc:	Exactly. In other words, as long as Heller likes.
Marianne:	That's not fair. Dad doesn't like internment.
Marc:	I should hope not.
Petra:	Of course not. He's a fine man.
Marc:	Rah, rah, rah. (*To Marianne*) Well, why did he do it, then? Why couldn't he leave them free, at least till they did something?

Marianne:	Because he daren't. If he'd –
Marc:	You've said it. He's afraid.
Petra:	You know it all, don't you?
Marianne	(*to Marc*): Do you mind if I finish what I was saying?
Marc:	Go on, then.
Marianne:	Dad daren't let them free, because he's afraid of riots.
Marc:	But he's causing riots. We'll be marching again on Thursday.
Marianne:	I'm not just talking about the university. If Dad let those communists free there'd be protest riots all over the country. Then the police would step in and you know what that means.
Petra:	Molluk.
Marc:	Well?
Marianne:	You'd say more than that if Molluk was in charge.
Marc:	Well, it could hardly be worse, could it?
Petra:	You're crazy. Can't you see any difference between Marianne's dad and the chief of police?
Marc:	Personally, there's a lot of difference. I don't agree with Heller, but I like talking to him. I've never met Molluk.
Marianne:	I wouldn't bother.
Petra:	It gives me the creeps just to see his photo.
Marc:	But that's not the point. A man can be OK as a bloke but still be wrong as Premier.
Petra:	Anyone would be wrong as Premier according to you – except your revolutionary society, of course.
Marianne:	But Marc, it is the police Dad's worried about. If there's big trouble and he goes, it won't be your lot that takes over.
Marc:	So he's tying himself in knots to save us from Molluk and keep everyone happy?
Petra:	What's wrong with keeping everyone happy?
Marc:	It doesn't work, that's what's wrong with it. You spend so much time trying to keep everyone happy that you forget what you were trying to do in the first place.
Marianne:	And you think that's happened to dad?
Marc:	It's possible.
Marianne:	Well, you'll have to put him straight tonight, won't you?
Marc:	Will it still be on, with this broadcast?
Marianne:	Oh yes. He'll do it from his study at home.
Marc:	Switching the public voice on and off – typical politician.
Marianne:	You don't have to come.
Marc:	No, I enjoy my little glimpses of power.

Marianne:	Sometimes I think you only go out with me because of dad's politics.
Marc:	I go out with you despite his politics, not because of them.
Petra:	Charming.
	(*Tomas, a member of the revolutionary society, enters and goes straight to Marc, ignoring the girls.*)
Tomas:	Marc? The committee want you, now. It's urgent.
Petra:	Like I said, charming.
Marc:	What's it about?
Tomas:	They'll tell you there. Are you coming?
Marc:	Sure. See you, Marianne. (*Marc goes out with Tomas.*)
Marianne	(*as he leaves*): See you.
Petra:	They make me sick – playing at politics.
Marianne:	Some of them are all right. I don't like everything Marc says, but I like it that he cares. I think Dad does, too.
Petra:	But I thought your Dad was going to control student societies.
Marianne:	I think he is, but he doesn't want to. He can't always do what he wants.
Petra:	Poor man, and on top of that he's got Marc coming to dinner.
Marianne:	Don't worry, we'll manage. (*Picking up books*) See you, Petra.
Petra:	See you. (*Marianne goes out.*)

Scene Two

The committee of the student revolutionary society meeting are seated in a small room in a rough semi-circle with Alex in the centre and Viktor beside him. Viktor sits calm and silent for most of the scene; it should be obvious from his clothes and manner that he isn't a member of the group.

Alex:	He's got to be stopped.
Carlo:	He's a hard man to persuade.
Alex:	I didn't say persuade – I said stopped.
Kristina:	But we had three thousand on the last march. How can you go against what three thousand people want?
Alex:	If you're Heller there's nothing easier. You just decide and to hell with the rest.
Jerome:	To hell with Heller – hey, what a slogan.
Andrei:	That's it – just one shot.

Kristina:	You mean kill him?
Andrei:	How else can you stop a politician who won't change his mind?
Carlo:	But how on earth . . .
Alex:	Look, Carlo, don't worry about how we do it. The main question is whether we do or not. I say we do.
Kristina:	But why?
Andrei:	Talk, talk, talk. Let's do something for a change.
Carlo:	But we're not going to kill Heller just to do something. (*Pause*) Well, are we?
Jerome:	Why not, it's better than lectures.
Alex:	Look, it's fairly simple. Heller became Premier as the man who was going to protect people's freedom and encourage education. Now we've got police spies on the campus and there's worse to come tonight.
Andrei:	He's sold out, that's all.
Carlo:	But other people have sold out.
Jerome:	Yes, far too many. That's why we stop this one.
Andrei:	All agreed?
Alex:	Kristina?
Kristina:	I don't . . . I don't know how you can do it. Just sit here and decide someone ought to die.
Jerome:	It's simple. Molluk does it all the time.
Carlo:	Well, that's great. We're supposed to be in favour of freedom and we end up copying the Chief of Police.
Andrei:	Whose side are you on?
Carlo:	The same as I always was. I want freedom, equal rights, for all the people.
Jerome:	Hallelujah, brother.
Andrei:	Blah, blah, blah.
Alex:	Shut up, this is serious. Kristina, what's worrying you?
Kristina:	Well . . . I don't think you can persuade people like Heller to change their minds. You've got to use pressure – that's why we had the march.
Andrei:	And why we hit back when Molluk's mob started.
Jerome:	Yeah, and when we hit we hit. (*Nudging Andrei*) That was one cop that didn't sleep too well, heh?
Alex:	Go on, Kristina?
Kristina:	Well . . . well, I just think . . . somehow, killing's different.
Viktor:	Surely, it's just another form of pressure.
Kristina:	Pretty drastic pressure.
Jerome:	It's a pretty drastic government.
Alex:	Kristina, I know you don't like it, but what else can we do? We haven't got much time. After tonight's broadcast we'll be finished. No meetings, no marches, no nothing.

Kristina:	Well, if it's that bad we'd have to do something.
Andrei:	Like what?
Kristina:	Well, we'd have to talk about it . . .
Max:	We'd still be talking when they locked us up. I say we get rid of him.
Carlo:	What happens when he's gone? After Heller, what next?
Jerome:	Who cares? It can't be worse.
Carlo:	It could be a lot worse. It could be Molluk.
Andrei:	He's got all he wants already.
Kristina:	I don't think so. I think Heller's stopped him a few times.
Carlo:	And if Heller goes and Molluk takes over, we're worse than we started.
Viktor:	You needn't fear Molluk.
Carlo:	Why not?
Viktor:	You needn't fear him.
Carlo:	How do you know? Just where do you fit in, anyway?
Alex:	Sorry, Carlo, you weren't here at the beginning. This is Viktor, from Hontal. They're in touch with the Northern group and their network. As soon as Heller goes they're ready to move in, and they've got contacts with the police so they can cope with Molluk.
Carlo:	If they're that organised, why do they need us?
Jerome:	What are you doing in a political society? Every time anything important comes up you want to get out of it.
Carlo:	I want things changed as much as you do. That's why I'm here.
Jerome	(*sarcastic*): Even if it means violence?
Carlo:	If it has to be violent, yes. Molluk's violent, the whole state's violent. But not just for the sake of it. Besides, I reckon I've done as much for this committee –
Alex:	We're not fighting about that. We know what we want. It's a question of how we get it.
Jerome:	And when.
Andrei:	Let's vote.
Carlo:	Couldn't we leave it, at least until after the broadcast?
Alex:	That may be too late. What happens if the broadcast bans us? We'd have had it.
Kristina:	But it seems so sudden. Out of nowhere. I mean, the sit-in and the march were OK, I could see the sense of them, but they didn't really hurt anyone.
Jerome:	Exactly, and nothing got changed. We've got a chance to really make a difference for once. Why not use it?
Alex:	Those in favour?
Kristina:	Wait a minute –
Alex:	Well, what do you want to do?

23

Kristina:	I don't know . . .
Jerome:	Exactly, and we do.
Carlo:	But even if we could do it –
Andrei:	We can do it.
Carlo:	How do we know it'll work?
Viktor:	You don't have to worry about what happens afterwards.
Carlo:	That's easy to say.
Viktor:	It's true.
Carlo:	How do we know it's true?
Viktor:	You just have to trust me.
Alex:	We can trust him. I can't tell you how I know – it's part of Viktor's security – but we can. Ok?
Carlo:	I don't like it.
Alex:	Those in favour? (*Alex, Jerome and Andrei raise their hands.*) Against? (*Carlo raises his hand, followed, less certainly, by Kristina. Viktor does nothing.*) Right, we do it.
Kristina:	But how?
Andrei:	I'll take care of it.
Alex:	Marc'll help, he's a member. But only this committee knows what's happening.
Carlo:	Is that the Marc that goes out with Heller's daughter?
Andrei:	That's the one.
Jerome:	Very convenient.
Carlo:	That's a bit rough, isn't it?
Jerome:	All's fair in love and war.
Andrei:	And this is war.
	(*A knock on the door, and Tomas enters.*)
Tomas:	OK, Alex?
Alex:	Yeah. Come in, Marc. Thanks, Tomas. (*Marc enters, Tomas goes out.*)
Marc:	What is it, some sort of demo?
Alex:	Not exactly. Heller's broadcast – will he do it from home?
Marc:	Yeah. I'll be there, hanging on every word.
Alex:	That's great. Could you do us a favour?
Marc:	Sure – unless you want me to poison his coffee. (*A joke that only he finds funny.*) He's giving me a meal, after all.
Alex:	All in the line of duty.
Jerome:	Oh, I wouldn't call Marianne Heller duty. Though, come to think of it –
Marc:	Have you got me here to listen to this creep?
Alex:	Jerome?
Jerome:	Yeah?
Alex:	Get out, will you?
Jerome:	Sure. (*As he goes*) Hey, no offence, mate.

Alex:	All we want is for you to get Andrei into Heller's house tonight. Andrei – you've met Marc?
	(*They nod briefly.*)
Andrei:	Nothing dramatic. Just some information we need.
Marc:	We're not going to stop the broadcast, then?
Andrei:	No, we thought we'd hear what he's got to say first. Right, Carlo?
Carlo:	Yeah, that's right.
Marc:	Oh, that's easy. I'll see Marianne, but there shouldn't be any problem.
Alex:	Fine. Thanks for the help. Sorry we can't go into more detail, but er . . .
Marc:	Fair enough, the way Molluk's snooping around.
Alex:	So – and this applies to all of us – no talking. OK? Nobody.
Andrei:	See you tonight then.
Marc:	Right. (*The meeting breaks up, and all go out.*)

Scene Three

An office in Police Headquarters, with Nilson busy at paper work. Molluk enters in a hurry.

Molluk:	Where is he?
Nilson:	I don't know, sir. Haven't seen him.
Molluk:	Korpov! Korpov!
Korpov	(*entering*): Sir?
Molluk:	Fetch me the broadcasting file, now. (*Korpov goes out.*) Right. All set for tonight?
Nilson:	Sir.
Molluk:	Don't forget, I want you there from 6.30 on, but I don't want you seen.
Nilson:	Sir.
Molluk:	Any questions?
Nilson:	Just one, sir. The student, sir, how do we know – (*He continues talking without realising that Korpov has returned. Molluk interrupts him fiercely.*)
Molluk:	What do you want, Korpov?
Korpov:	The file, sir. (*He hands it over. Molluk takes it, and flicks angrily through the papers in it.*)
Molluk:	Well, where's the security map?
Korpov:	You didn't . . . In the map office, sir.
Molluk:	Well, I need it, don't I? Don't I?
Korpov:	I don't know, sir. Do you?

25

Molluk:	I've just told you I do. Fetch it, Korpov, immediately. (*Korpov leaves.*) Nilson, you should know better. I have made it quite clear that I do not want this matter discussed. Not in front of anyone.
Nilson:	Sorry, sir. For a moment I'd forgotten that –
Molluk:	There is only one mistake, and that is forgetting. Don't forget. Remember what you have to do, and whose side you're on. Mine. Not Heller's, not Korpov's, but mine. Remember?
Nilson:	Yes, sir.
Molluk:	Now, what was your question?
Nilson:	How can we be sure what the student will do, sir?
Molluk:	You can't be sure. I can, so you'll just have to trust me. Right?
Nilson:	Yes, sir.
Molluk:	Good. Keep to your orders. Korpov!
Korpov	(*returning*): Sir?
Molluk:	Well? The map?
Korpov:	The map section don't have it, sir. They . . . well, they say you collected it this morning.
Molluk:	Well, it'll be in my office, won't it?
Korpov:	Yes, sir.
Molluk:	So I won't need it. (*He prepared to go, but suddenly remembers a further detail.*) Oh, Korpov, I'll want you on alert from 6.00 pm tonight.
Korpov:	It was my evening off, sir. I'd promised the wife –
Molluk:	So it was. Well, from 6.00 pm. Here. One of our agents has asked for an assault squad and a van. You'll be told where later.
Korpov:	But . . . sir . . .
Molluk:	Yes?
Korpov:	Nothing, sir. No questions.
Molluk:	That's good. Very good. (*Molluk goes out, leaving Korpov staring after him, while Nilson goes back to his paper work.*)

Scene Four

A room in the college, as in Scene One. Marianne is reading, as Marc approaches.

Marc:	Marianne?
Marianne:	Don't tell me you've got time off from the revolution actually to talk to me.
Marc:	Don't start that again.

Marianne:	So what was the big, secret meeting about?
Marc:	I don't know. It wasn't that clear.
Marianne:	All that fuss and security. It's worse than Molluk. And when you do get down to it – nothing. Just a load of talk. It's not surprising people like Petra have no time for them.
Marc:	You can't run a political society just to please people like Petra. She wouldn't be interested anyway.
Marianne:	You don't know that.
Marc:	We haven't got the time to find out.
Marianne:	But it's people like her you're up against. It's her sort you've got to convince. Like Dad says, you can't win if you only talk to your friends.
Marc:	If I talked to Petra for long I'd end up forgetting what I wanted to say. She thinks politics is just a hobby for people who like that sort of thing.
Marianne:	It's all right for you. You know what you care about, what you'd like to change. It's not easy for her to see the point of it.
Marc:	But you do.
Marianne:	I haven't got any choice.
Marc:	That sounds bitter.
Marianne:	I am bitter. Going round college and just hearing people muttering at you, never straight out, just a mutter and a look, daring you to ask what they've just said.
Marc:	Well, you can hardly expect them to like your dad.
Marianne:	I'm not asking them to like him. I'm asking them to leave me out.
Marc:	But you're involved.
Marianne:	And don't I know it. You're just like Dad – 'Politics is everyone's business. Politics is too important to leave to the politicians . . . de dah de dah de dah.' Well, just for a few minutes I'd like to bury myself in a corner and let the lot of you go to hell.
Marc:	What?
Marianne:	Yes, and especially you and your lousy socialist society. So full of building peace and freedom in the future that you don't leave us any peace or freedom now. (*Pause*) I've just had enough, that's all. I'll see you tonight.
Marc:	Can I bring someone?
Marianne:	Who?
Marc:	He's called Andrei.
Marianne:	Who? You've never mentioned him before.
Marc:	I don't know him that well, but he's keen to meet your dad.

Marianne:	Watch the animals feeding, is that it?
Marc:	All right, I'll tell him not to come.
Marianne:	No, he can come.
Marc:	Don't bother.
Marianne:	Oh, bring him. It's just that Molluk gets touchy if we have strangers around.
Marc:	Aren't I a stranger?
Marianne:	You don't count. I told him you were harmless.
Marc:	Well, thanks.
Marianne:	Don't mention it. You'll just have to wait a bit longer at the gate, that's all. Oh, just one thing.
Marc:	Yeah?
Marianne:	Promise you won't take over the broadcast – I couldn't stand a meal arguing about what you were going to tell the country.
Marc:	All right, I promise. See you tonight.
Marianne:	See you. (*Marc goes, Marianne continues reading.*)

Scene Five

The students' committee room, as in Scene Two, but the atmosphere this time is much more disorderly. They are meeting at short notice, with some excitement.

Jerome:	What's up?
Carlo:	There's Molluk's men all over the place.
Jerome:	Have we changed our minds, or something?
Kristina:	I wish we had.
Carlo:	What is it, Alex?
Alex:	Will you all shut up a minute and listen? They've been into the office, checking up on all sorts of things, and they've asked for Andrei's file.
Jerome:	So? They've got nothing on Andrei except the April demo, and that was legal.
Carlo:	That's not the point. Why Andrei?
Jerome:	He's a good bloke. If I were Molluk I'd want to know about Andrei.
Carlo:	The point is, why should they check on Andrei now?
Alex:	Exactly. Why today? Who's decided it's a good time to check on Andrei?
Jerome:	Any suggestions – Carlo?
Carlo:	How the hell should I know? I'm getting a bit sick of this –

Alex:	All right, that's enough.
Carlo:	Just because you're clever and nasty enough to run the newspaper doesn't mean you run the college.
Jerome:	Sure, Carlo, sure.
Carlo:	And just because I don't agree with killing Heller doesn't mean I'd put Molluk onto it. Besides, if I'd wanted to bust Andrei I'd have done it by now, wouldn't I?
Jerome:	So who is it?
Kristina:	Well, I think we should rule out everyone here.
Jerome:	But who else knew about Andrei?
Carlo:	Marc?
Alex:	Marc doesn't know why Andrei's going. Anyway, he's been a member for years.
Jerome:	What about Heller's daughter?
Carlo:	She'll only just have heard, and she won't know anything about Andrei. What about that Viktor? Where did you say he was from?
Alex:	Up North. Near Hontal.
Carlo:	Well?
Kristina:	It's got to be.
Alex:	No, it can't be him. He's right at the top of their organisation – he took a hell of a risk in coming here. He knew everything about everybody. He must be one of their top people.
Jerome:	Perhaps the Hontal people are jealous.
Carlo:	Of us?
Jerome:	Why not?
Carlo:	What have we done to be jealous of? They won't have heard of us.
Alex:	And killing Heller would help them anyway, so it can't be that.
Kristina:	So, who can it be?
Alex:	I don't know. We'll have to leave it for now, but be careful.
Jerome:	Andrei's the one who wants to be careful.
Carlo:	Now that's one job I wouldn't have.
Jerome:	Scared?
Carlo:	Sure. Wouldn't you be? A gun in your pocket and a chance to kill the Premier. God, I'd be . . .
Kristina:	It makes me ill just thinking about it.
Jerome:	You needn't worry about Andrei. Whoever else is sweating, it won't be him.
Kristina:	He can't have any feelings.
Alex:	Sometimes you need people like that, to do the dirty work.
Carlo:	Dirty is right.

Jerome:	So nice people like Carlo can have a clean conscience.
Carlo:	What d'you mean? I'm in this as deep as you are.
Alex:	We're all in it. Every one of us. (*They go out.*)

Scene Six

The staging of this scene needs to be flexible, as it moves rapidly from place to place, and there should be the minimum of delay in movement from one area to another. Continuity of action is far more important than detailed scenery.

(A) Marianne and Mrs. Heller prepare for the meal. A tray of drinks is ready on the side. Mrs. Heller seems anxious.

Marianne:	Stop worrying, mother. Everything's all right.
Mrs. Heller:	Yes, but I have to make sure it is.
Marianne:	Come on, sit down. It's only Marc – oh, and that friend of his.
Mrs. Heller:	That may be all we've got to feed, but your father's got this infernal broadcast to do. Oh, I wish . . .
Marianne:	What?
Mrs. Heller:	I wish we didn't always have our life interrupted. Just now and again it would be nice to sit down to an ordinary meal.
Marianne:	You wish Dad wasn't Premier?
Mrs. Heller:	Not really. He wanted to do it, and there are a lot worse who might be running the country.
Marianne:	D'you think he'll ever retire?
Mrs. Heller:	I don't know. He talks about it sometimes, but there's always another crisis.
Marianne:	Like us students stirring it up?
Mrs. Heller:	Well, it might be a joke to you, but your father's not finding it funny.
Heller	(*entering, holding a copy of his speech*): What don't I find funny?
Mrs. Heller:	These student riots.
Marianne:	But you said yourself you wouldn't want them to be quiet and peaceful. I'll bet you caused enough trouble when you were young.
Heller:	Oh, I stirred things up quite a bit.
Mrs. Heller:	But you weren't at college. You were working at the quarries.

Heller:	Only because I had to be.
Mrs. Heller:	And the government was a lot worse. That Banning, he was a real dictator – now he was someone worth fighting.
Heller:	Don't you think I'm worth fighting?
Mrs. Heller:	Don't be silly, Erik.
Marianne:	There's plenty who do. Marc's society in college hate your guts.
Heller:	Quite right too. If I were a student, I'd agree with them.
Mrs. Heller:	That's your trouble – you're too soft. I don't like Molluk, but I think he's right about the students. They need a bit of discipline before they do something really dangerous. Now it would be all right if they just talked about politics, but –
Heller:	If I were a student that really would make me mad. These are clever people who care about how things are – why shouldn't they be allowed to act as well as talk?
Marianne:	You sound just like Marc.
Heller:	In a lot of ways I think I am.
Mrs. Heller:	But you didn't become Premier just by marching down a street, throwing bricks through windows and shouting slogans.
Heller:	Of course, getting into power takes time, and when you're young you don't want to wait for anything. Anyway, they'll be angrier still when they hear about this lot (*tapping script*).
Marianne:	Oh, the Premier's broadcast. Can I have a look, Dad?
Heller:	No, love, sorry. Top security. Still, in half an hour the whole country will know, and I'm afraid your Marc won't be that happy.

(B) Marc and Andrei, waiting at a guard post outside Heller's home.

Marc:	I usually get straight through, but it'll take a bit longer while they check on you at the house.
Andrei:	Very efficient. What's Heller like, then?
Marc:	Nice bloke, personally.
Andrei:	But a sod in power, eh?
Marc:	Seems like it. But it's dificult to believe when you meet him.
Andrei:	Oldest trick in the book, that. Put on the manners, talk nice and keep smiling, and you get away with murder.
Marc:	Strange, though, 'cos he wasn't born to it.
Andrei:	Yeah, my dad told me. Heller's dad was a navvy – left school early and all the old sob story, pulled himself up by his bootstraps.

31

Marc:	It takes something to get on like that.
Andrei:	And then turn round and stab your own people in the back. My dad watched Heller on the way up, thought he was great. Then as soon as he's really in power, what does he do? Laws against the unions, no more houses built, police everywhere. He's like the rest, just out for what he can get.
Marc:	Can't be easy, though, changing the whole system.
Andrei:	I wouldn't mind if he tried. But he's just talk. He talks about justice and equality, but everything he does is against us. (*Pause*)
Marc:	Why are you coming?
Andrei:	Eh?
Marc:	You said you wanted to meet Heller. It sounds as though you've made up your mind already.
Andrei:	I know what I think. I just wanted to hear what he's got to say.
Marc:	But it won't change your mind?
Andrei:	Of course not. He hasn't changed yours, has he?
Marc:	No, but . . .
Andrei:	Look, you do all right. Nice girl, good family, money coming in and a nice safe job ahead of you. Where I come from, there's three brothers and two sisters waiting for brother Andrei to bring something home. Their dad's not going to recover from working in the quarries, their mum could break down any day, and friend Heller's government isn't going to lift a finger.
Marc:	But you're not going to change his mind tonight.
Andrei:	Maybe not.
Marc:	So why come?
Andrei:	I've got my reasons.
Marc:	Hey, the guard's waving us on. Come on, and don't throw any bombs till we've had a drink.
Andrei:	Don't worry about me, I'll behave myself.

(C) Set as for (A), inside Heller's house, as Marc and Andrei arrive.

Mrs. Heller:	Hello, Marc, do come in.
Marc:	Mrs. Heller – this is Andrei Kotzal.
Mrs. Heller:	Pleased to meet you. You're at the college, too, I suppose? (*Andrei shakes hands and nods.*)
Marianne:	That's it. The house is full of revolutionaries.
Heller:	Hello, Marc, good to see you. And this is –
Marc:	Andrei Kotzal.
Heller:	How d'you do? And are you politically minded?
Andrei:	You could say that.

Heller:	You're from the north?
Andrei:	Guldanna.
Heller:	Really? I was born three miles from there, at Hontal.
Andrei:	Yes, my father told me.
Heller:	He's in the quarries, then?
Andrei:	He was. His back went.
Heller:	Yes, it's hard there. I . . .
Andrei:	Well?
Heller:	Yes?
Andrei:	Forget it.
Heller:	No, it's important. You want to know why I don't do something about it, don't you? Why don't I order the firms to pay compensation, or take over the quarries?
Andrei:	Something like that.
Heller:	That's what we planned, when we started. I'd still like to, but –
Mrs. Heller:	Erik, it's time for the broadcast.
Heller:	Really? Oh, I'd better go and do this thing, but we'll talk when I come back. Have another drink. I shan't be long. (*Goes out.*)
Andrei:	Huh. Typical politician.
Marianne:	Be fair. He's got to do the broadcast.
Marc:	Yes, and what is it? Some announcement crippling the student unions, and we're here drinking wine next door. It's crazy.
Marianne:	What d'you want to do, take over and announce a revolution?
Mrs. Heller:	Not tonight, thankyou very much.
Marianne:	And you did promise to behave yourself. Besides, I don't think you'd get far. Molluk's discreet, but his men are all over the place.
Andrei:	Yeah. I bet he holds the microphone for the broadcast.
Marianne:	Don't be silly.
Mrs. Heller:	You're very clever, aren't you? It's all so easy. My husband was born in the north and he doesn't do what you want, so he's a traitor. He has to watch Molluk, so that makes him a coward. If only you knew . . .
Andrei:	Go on.
Mrs. Heller:	I can't tell you. Half of it's guesses, and –
Andrei:	Just trust the top man and we'll all be OK. Here we go again.
Marianne:	Are you really a friend of Marc's?
Andrei:	Sure. Well, Marc?
Marc	(*uneasy*): Yeah, Marianne . . . er . . . he's OK. Like your dad, he says what he thinks, but he's got a point. How can we be expected to understand when so much is secret?

33

Marianne:	You can talk. What about your society committee?
Andrei:	That's different. We're not running the country.
Mrs. Heller:	No, and thank God for that.
Marianne:	And you're wrong about Molluk. Dad does the broadcast on his own in the study. He won't have anyone else there. Just him and a microphone.
Andrei:	I see.
Mrs. Heller:	Will you have some more wine?
Marc:	Yeah, thanks.
Andrei:	No thanks. If you'll excuse me . . . um . . . er . . .
Mrs. Heller:	It's down that corridor, past the study and then on the left.
Andrei:	Thanks. I can manage. (*Goes out, closing the door behind him.*)
Marianne:	Can't you get him to tone it down a bit?
Marc:	Your dad didn't seem to mind.
Mrs. Heller:	Well, I'm afraid I do. I don't know what you think gives you the right to tell the rest of the world what to do, but I've had quite enough of it. If that young man doesn't mend his manners by the time he comes back he can go home to his college.
Marianne:	Marc, why is he here?
Marc:	I told you. He wants to talk to your dad.
Marianne:	Well, he's got a funny way of doing it.

(D) In one part of the stage, Heller alone preparing to deliver his broadcast, checking script and adjusting position of microphone. In another, the college committee in a dark room, gathered to hear the announcement.

Heller:	People of Durium, I apologise for interrupting your normal listening, but I have an announcement to make that will, I think, concern you all. You will, I am sure, have followed reports of the unrest in many colleges of our republic. I recognise that it is right for our young people to be interested in political affairs –
Jerome:	Thanks very much.
Heller:	. . . indeed, I can well remember my own days as a lad in the quarries –
Jerome:	Here we go. Sob story again.
Heller:	– but in Hontal we knew the difference between agitation and violence.
Alex:	Surprise, surprise.
Jerome:	Tut, tut, violence again. Sermon coming up.
Carlo:	Shut up.

Heller:	. . . and when expensive property is being damaged it is time for your government to act.
Alex:	Here it comes.
Jerome:	Heller's last words.
Kristina:	Stop talking like that, will you?
Heller:	From now until the end of the current crisis, it will be illegal for the students of state universities to hold political meetings and any infringement of this law will lead to expulsion or – in severe cases – imprisonment.
Jerome:	Why not just shoot the lot of us?
Alex:	Hang on, he hasn't finished yet.
Heller:	I realise that these measures may seem harsh, and I assure you that I take them with no great enjoyment –
Jerome:	Not much.
Heller:	– but I regard them as necessary for the good of the country.
Alex:	Turn it off. (*Kristina does so. Outside, the blast of a whistle.*)
Kristina:	What was that?
	(*Korpov enters, armed, with other policemen, followed by Viktor. He walks slowly and calmly, as if amused by the whole business.*)
Viktor:	It's all right. They won't be armed.
Alex:	Viktor, what is this?
Viktor:	Come along then, everybody.
Jerome:	You crummy sod – (*Jerome tries to hit Viktor, but is held by a policeman and stopped by Korpov's gun. Viktor hits Jerome coolly and hard.*)
Viktor:	You'll cool down in jail. All right, Korpov, to security. We'll interrogate them later. They don't know much.

(E) Heller's study, at the moment when he finishes the announcement.

Heller:	I realise that these measures may seem harsh, and I assure you I take them with no great enjoyment, but I regard them as necessary for the good of the country. (*He switches off the microphone and sits, thoughtful, as Andrei approaches from the shadows.*)
Andrei:	You do, do you?
Heller:	Yes, I'm afraid I do. I didn't think you'd like it.
Andrei:	Nor will you. (*Takes out a small gun from his pocket.*)
Heller:	And what will that do?
Andrei:	Get rid of you.
Heller:	And then what?
Andrei:	A chance of some honest government. We might see some change in this rotten country.

Heller:	All you'll see is Molluk.
Andrei:	He runs it anyway.
Heller:	Not yet he doesn't. But he will if you kill me. That would be just the excuse he wants to stamp down on your movement.
Andrei:	What about your broadcast? Isn't that stamping down?
Heller:	That's a gift. A present to Molluk – to stop him taking over.
Andrei:	A compromise.
Heller:	Yes, if you like.
Andrei:	I don't like. It stinks. You've betrayed your own people.
Heller:	Well, go ahead and shoot me, if you know all the answers.
Andrei:	What?
Heller:	Shoot me. Unless you're scared, of course. Don't you see, the whole thing's much bigger than you are. It seems easy, but you won't change a thing. You'll make it worse.
Andrei:	Shut up.
Heller:	You don't know what you're doing. You're playing a dirty game, but you don't know the rules. You're bound to lose, you – (*Andrei shoots Heller and watches him collapse. Andrei stands horrified as Nilson emerges quietly. He shoots Andrei calmly in the back.*)
Molluk	(*entering quietly*): Everything all right?
Nilson:	Yes, sir. Just as you said. Took his time, though.
Molluk	(*picks up the phone and speaks into it*): Hello? Broadcasting Service? Molluk here. I want that tape putting out in two minutes from now. Of course I'm sure. Listen, you take orders from me from now on. Is that understood?
	(*Marc runs in, looks at the two bodies and stares.*)
Marc:	What's happened? Who are you?
Molluk:	You needn't worry. It's taken care of. Go back to your dinner.
Marc:	But they're dead. What's happened?
Molluk:	I don't think you really want to know.
Marc:	I . . . I . . . brought him here.
Molluk:	Never mind, we'll cover that up. Go back to the girl. She'll need looking after now her father's dead.
Marc:	But –
Nilson:	Out. (*Marc, shattered, goes out.*)
Molluk:	We've got the rest, have we?
Nilson:	Yes, sir. Korpov radioed in five minutes ago.
Molluk:	Good. (*Into phone*) Right, broadcast now. (*As Molluk*

36

and Nilson look round and slowly go out, there is the sound of an announcer's voice. The two bodies remain visible on the stage.)

Announcer: We interrupt Music by Night to bring you an urgent announcement. President Erik Heller has just been assassinated at his home by revolutionary students. The assassin was shot attempting escape, and all parties to the plot are being held for interrogation. The Commissioner of Police, Colonel Molluk, will act as Premier during the present crisis. All measures essential for security will be taken, for the good of the country.

Changes in the Air

Mr. Adam Slaney, *a nailer*
Will ⎫
Jem ⎬ *his sons*
Arthur ⎭
Mrs. Susan Slaney, *Adam's wife*
Ellen, *their daughter*
Grandmother, *Susan's mother*
Richard Miller
John Watson
Arnold, *Innkeeper of 'The Angel'*
Ephraim Ward

Visitor, *working for Jedediah Strutt*
Polly, *a mushroom seller*
Robert Blincowe, *a runaway*
Jenks ⎫ *overseers at Litton*
Sam ⎬ *mill*
Oliver, *a government spy*
Jeremiah Brandreth, *a radical*
Samuel Hunt, *a Pentrich farmer*
Isaac Ludlam, *a lay preacher*
Miss Price, *a school-teacher*

There are also orphan children, mill workers, children at the school, and guests at the final celebration.

The play takes place in Belper, Derbyshire, starting in 1775.

Scene One

The life is hard as iron rods
When nailing is your trade,
You curse the Lord when there's no work
And praise him when you're paid;
One day you're drunk, the next you starve
There's no two weeks the same,
But that's the way it's always been
'Cos that's the nailing game.

The Slaney cottage, small, simple and slightly cramped, with a nailshop attached. Mrs. Slaney is cooking, Ellen combing her hair and Grandmother in her chair. Mr. Slaney enters from the nailshop.

Mr. Slaney:	Where're my rods?
Ellen:	I haven't seen 'em, father.
Mr. Slaney:	Where're my rods? I had 'em not five minutes ago.
Grandmother:	It's cold in here.
Mr. Slaney:	I get fifty pounds of rods a week, and if there aren't forty-five pounds of nails I'll get short wages.
Mrs. Slaney:	We've not had your rods, Adam. Can you not get some more wood? You can see my mother's cold.
Mr. Slaney:	If I don't get these nails made she'll stay cold. (*Arthur runs, in holding the rods. He sees Adam, and tries to run out, but Adam grabs him.*) Got you! Had 'em again, have you? I told you last time – you take those rods and I'll end up in court. (*Adam hits him.*)
Arthur:	There's only four.
Mr. Slaney:	That's four too many. I've told you before – keep out of the nailshop.
Arthur:	Will's in there.
Mr. Slaney:	Will's making nails, he's earning something.
Arthur:	Well, I'll make nails, then.
Ellen:	You? You're not strong enough to make a pin.
Arthur:	Well, what do you do, then? Look at yourself in a mirror day-dreaming all the time.
Ellen:	I've fed the pigs. (*Arthur snorts.*)
Mrs. Slaney:	That's enough bickering from you two.
Mrs. Slaney:	I don't care what you get up to – just stay out of the nailshop, that's all. (*He goes out, as Jem enters from outside.*)
Jem:	What's up?
Mrs. Slaney:	Nothing to fret about, Jem.
	(*Jem unloads a small bag of coal into the grate.*)
Grandmother:	Is that all you could get?
Jem:	You can get some more yourself if you fancy it, grandmother. It's not easy work, digging coal.
Mrs. Slaney:	No work's easy.
Grandmother:	That's right enough.
Jem:	All right, don't go on. I'm just saying, that's all I can get today. If you want more, someone else'll have to get it.
Arthur:	Is supper ready yet?
Mrs. Slaney:	It's ready when I tell you, and not before.
Arthur:	What is it?
Mrs. Slaney:	Hasty pudding.
Arthur:	Again?
Mrs. Slaney:	At least we can afford it.
Mr. Slaney	(*re-entering*): At the moment we can, 'cos they need nails. What's going to happen if the winter's bad, though?

Ellen:	When I'm older I shan't have hasty pudding.
Arthur:	You're a deal too fat as it is.
Ellen	(*pulls Arthur's hair, then stops*): No, I shall marry some nice gentleman and we shall dine on meat every day.
Mrs. Slaney:	And what rich lord's going to take a fancy to you, do you think?
Ellen:	I haven't decided yet.
Mrs. Slaney:	Well, you can decide to get this pudding served out. Ellen, tell our Will that his supper's ready. (*Ellen goes out to nailshop.*) Come on now, mother, Arthur. (*They sit round to eat.*)
Jem:	What'll our Ellen do, then, till she finds her gentleman?
Mrs. Slaney:	She talks of being a governess or a teacher.
Jem:	Our Ellen? She can barely read and write.
Grandmother:	She's a bright girl, and a sight nearer being educated than you'll ever be, Jem Slaney.
Jem:	Oh, she's bright enough, but how'll she ever get to be a school teacher?
Ellen	(*returning with Will*): Never you mind, brother Jem, how I'll manage it.
Will:	There's a school at Cromford, started by Mister Strutt, that owns the mill.
Mr. Slaney:	I don't know, about him or his mill, and I don't want to know.
Will:	From all I hear, he's a fine man.
Ellen:	And they say his son George is even finer. A proper gentleman.
Jem:	Well, you can keep your proper gentleman – and his machines. He's not getting me working for him.
Ellen:	I shouldn't think he'd want you.
Will:	I shouldn't mind working for them, you know.
Mr. Slaney:	You're not going to Cromford. I need you here.
Will:	But there's others – and the mill pays well.
Jem:	You'll not catch me working in the nailshop all day.
Arthur:	I'll help, father.
Ellen:	You couldn't lift the hammer.
Mrs. Slaney:	Well, you can all stop squabbling and finish your pudding, since it's there and it's all you'll get.
Jem:	Not to worry. We'll make up for it Monday, Saint Monday. Time for a holiday.
Mr. Slaney:	It's been a long wait for it this time.
Grandmother:	When I were a girl, if trade was good, we'd have Saint Monday, Tuesday and Wednesday – no nails made for three days – and a fair few heads broken, too.
Ellen:	A whole lot of drinking and brawling. I think it's common.

Will:	What d'you mean, common? It's the custom.
Mr. Slaney:	It's there, and you can't change it.

Saint Monday Song

If you don't like interruptions to disturb the general calm,
If you fancy entertainment but don't wish to come to harm,
If you don't want fractured fingers or a dislocated arm,
    Then stay clear of Belper nailers on Saint Monday.

You won't come to harm in Derbyshire in most days of the year,
On a Belper Sunday morning you won't find a lot to fear,
But there's one time in the year when you'd be better off not here
    Stay away from Belper nailers on Saint Monday.

Scene Two

The Angel, Belper. Richard Miller and John Watson, both regulars, are playing dominoes. Ephraim Ward, a local eccentric, leans against the bar, drinking alone. A visitor, looking lost but friendly, approaches Arnold, the landlord.

Visitor:	Good day to you, innkeeper.
Arnold:	Morning.
Visitor:	Pray tell me, are you the only tavern in Belper?
	(*Raucous laughter from John, Richard and Ephraim.*)
Arnold:	No, sir.
Ephraim:	Not the only one, sir, but the best. Right, Arnold?
Arnold:	That's right, Ephraim. Here, you're nearly empty.
Visitor:	But I understood that there were only six hundred people resident in Belper?
Arnold:	That's right, sir, but they're nailers, you see.
Richard:	Thirsty work, making nails. Right, John?
John:	Oh, er . . . right. Ay, well. Two more, then, Arnold.
Visitor:	But you're not working today?
Ephraim:	Not on Saint Monday, sir. (*Visitor stares politely, as Ephraim attempts to explain.*) It's the nailer's holiday . . . you see, sir . . . well, that is . . . (*he gives up*).

Visitor:	Oh, how interesting. And, er . . . what happens?
Arnold:	You'll see soon enough, sir.
	(*The sound of screams and yells as a gang of children run in, fighting, pushing and shoving.*) Watch your purse, sir. Go on, get out of it! (*The children make faces at the adults, and start to run out. Richard catches one and clouts him, while the rest run out. Richard and John return to their dominoes, which have been disturbed.*)
Richard:	Right, my turn.
John:	Now, I'd not be certain, but . . .
Ephraim	(*interfering*): Well, I'd say that was there, and . . .
Richard:	Get out of it.
Ephraim:	I was only trying to help, I just . . .
Richard:	Ephraim Ward, that's my money and you're not having it.
	(*Mr. Slaney, Will and Jem enter, look at John and Richard, and then go to the bar.*)
Richard:	Well, it's Adam Slaney. I thought you'd be working today.
Mr. Slaney:	Me, work on Saint Monday?
Jem:	Good Saint Monday to you, Mr. Watson.
John:	Now just you mind your tongue, young Jem or I might have to crack your head for you again.
Mr. Slaney:	Let's get some ale down before we fight.
Richard:	I'll drink to that. We'll fight later.
Visitor:	Good day, gentlemen. And might I ask if you are nailers?
Jem:	I'm no nailer. I dig coal.
Mr. Slaney:	We're nailers, sir. Why d'you ask?
Visitor:	I wondered if I might interest you in a proposition.
Ephraim:	I don't know about a porposition, you could interest me in a pint of ale.
Richard:	Hear, hear.
Jem:	That's right, Ephraim.
Visitor	(*embarrassed, but eager to do the right thing*): Oh . . . er . . . yes, of course. Very well. Landlord, a pint of ale for everyone here – and one for yourself.
Arnold:	Thankyou, sir. You're most generous.
Richard:	Handsome of you, mister. What's your business?
Visitor:	I am an associate of Mr. Jedediah Strutt of Derby. Perhaps you know of him?
Mr. Slaney:	Too well.
Richard:	We're nailers. We're not going to Cromford.
Visitor:	That won't be necessary. Mr. Strutt will be coming to you, as it were.
John:	I don't quite follow your meaning, sir . . .
Visitor:	Mr. Strutt is to build a mill here at Belper. Permit me.

(*He unfolds a large public notice for them to read. For a time they pretend to understand it, but then give up.*)

Mr. Slaney: If you'd be good enough to explain, sir. We're not that familiar with notices here.

Visitor (*reading*): 'Wanted, at Belper, in the county of Derby, Joiners and Carpenters, Knitters and Weavers, with large families. Children of all ages, above seven years old, may have constant employment. Young men may have trades taught them, which will enable them to maintain a family in a short time. By personal application at the mill particulars may be known.'

Jem: You'll not catch me in a mill.

Will: It's good, steady work, and well paid. Are there chances for advancement?

Visitor: Oh indeed. A young man if he's bright and keen, could be appointed overseer, manager, director, even. There's no limit to his progress.

Richard: Progress, you call it. Not much progress for the nailers.

Mr. Slaney: No offence, sir, but I like to be my own man. I don't want an overseer telling me when to work.

Will: But you have to get the nails made, all the same.
(*Polly enters with basket of mushrooms.*)

Polly: Mushrooms, mushrooms.

John: Ah, now come here, Miss Polly.

Polly: D'you want some mushrooms, then?

John: No. Just come over here.

Polly: Oh, no fear. Mushrooms, mushrooms. (*To visitor*) Sir?

Visitor: Er, no thankyou, miss, er . . .

Jem: Here, Polly, I'll have a few.

Polly: Why, that's very good of you, master Jem.

Jem (*pretending to pick carefully*): I'll have that one . . . and that one . . . and that one (*he pinches her bottom; Polly squeals and runs out*).

Mr. Slaney: What'll help the nail business, then, when the mill comes?

Visitor: Mr. Strutt wishes only to make cloth. There'll be no competition.

Richard: Ah, that's what you say now.

Will: I think you're frightened, Mr. Miller.

Richard: Frightened? Are you calling me frightened, young Will? I'll show you who's frightened. (*Rolls up his sleeves.*)

Visitor: Gentlemen, please, there's no call for fisticuffs. I don't wish to . . .

Arnold: Don't you worry, sir, it's just his way. There's no malice.

John:	Ay, if you think that's rough you should have seen the old days. You recall that football game at Duffield, Adam? They paid Obadiah Flint to play bad, and by the time we'd lost, there was hell to pay. You've never seen owt like it. Broken legs, bruises, skulls cracked – that were a day, eh Adam?
Mr. Slaney:	Right enough.
Jem	(*looking through the door*): Watch 'em, here they come. (*The children rush in again, in a riot, and leave, watched by the adults.*)
Visitor:	But . . . er . . . who are these ragamuffins? They're not your sons, I take it?
Richard:	Sons? Them our sons? (*Ephraim points at Richard, and laughs loudly.*) Shut up, you drunken lout or I'll stuff your pintpot down your throat.
Will:	They're the orphans.
Visitor:	From Belper?
Jem:	Some say they're from Milford.
Richard:	And in Milford they say they're from Belper.
John:	Ah, but there's no one wants 'em round here.
Mr. Slaney:	Lads that young are no good for nailing.
John:	Half of 'em 'd steal your tools soon as look at you.
Visitor:	Steal? They steal, do they? (*He gazes in wonder, and then starts to search his pockets for his purse.*) My purse, it's vanished. Where is it? (*He looks round anxiously, but they all stare back at him. Frantically, he runs out.*) Come back, you young rascals, come back this minute.
Will:	One minute, sir. (*Goes after him.*)
Ephraim:	That's him gone. (*He puts on a posh voice, to imitate the visitor.*) Well, gentlemen, perhaps I could interest you in a porposition? (*Laughter*) Let's drink to Mr. Strutt and his merry men.

My lord has entered, my oh my,
He speaks with accents rare,
His perfume spirals through the sky
There's changes in the air:
But can't you hear the children cry
Their nerves and clothing tear
They're pumping smoke into the sky
There's changes in the air.

Scene Three

Open ground, not far from the Slaney cottage. Arthur wandering around, hears someone approach and hides. Robert Blincowe enters, warily.

Arthur: Are you going to steal something?
Robert: Who are you?
Arthur: Arthur. I live here. Who are you?
Robert: Robert Blincowe – but if you tell anyone, I'll kill you.
Arthur: You sound desperate.
Robert: I am. I mean it.
Arthur: We'll see (*Arthur makes a grab at Robert. They fight, but Robert cries out, holding his hand. Arthur stops.*) You didn't last long.
Robert: My hand. You got my hand.
Arthur: Huh. I hadn't started.
Robert: It wasn't you. I did it before. Look.
Arthur: Ugh – there's a bit missing.
Robert: I know. I caught it in the machine.
Arthur: Does it hurt?
Robert: Not much.
Arthur: Where are you from?
Robert: Litton.
Arthur: But that's twenty miles away.
Robert: I know. I've been walking since Saturday.
Arthur: It's taken you two days to get here?
Robert: I had to be careful.
Arthur: Why? What have you done?
Robert: Can you keep your mouth shut? (*Arthur nods*) I've run away from Mr. Needham's mill at Litton. His men are after me.
Arthur: But if you don't want to work –
Robert: Want to? Huh, I've got to. I'm apprenticed till I'm twenty-one. I was sold to Mr. Needham last year, to work at the mill.
Arthur: What about your family?
Robert: Got none.
Arthur: So where will you go?
Robert: Dunno. You'll not tell anyone?
Arthur: Course not. What'll happen if they catch you?
Robert: I'll get beaten again.
Arthur: What else do they beat you for?
Robert: Not working, fighting, talking out of turn.
Arthur: And what d'you have to do?

Robert:	I'll tell you. (*A chorus of mill children start a mime as Robert explains.*) Bell goes at five o'clock, and governor goes round with his whip, so we all get dressed, quick. When the hatch door opens –
Arthur:	What do you get, hasty pudding?
Robert:	I wish we did. Black bread and porridge, and not much of it. Then, at 5.30, work. (*Children mime the loom.*) The power loom. It's big and heavy, and it makes a lot of cloth. There's warp threads and weft threads; the warp threads go up and down, and the weft thread goes across, and we have to keep it working.
Arthur:	What do you do?
Robert:	Well, what do we do?
Chorus:	If the thread breaks, tie it.
Arthur:	But the loom is always moving.
Robert:	Does it stop?
Chorus:	No.
Robert:	If there's loose ends –
Chorus:	Cut them off.
Arthur:	But the loom is always moving.
Robert:	Does it stop?
Chorus:	No –
	Got to keep it moving
	Oil the wheels
	But not the thread
	Give out the reels
	Earn your bread
	Unload the bales
	Tie loose ends
	Wash the pails
	All hours God sends
Arthur:	But how long does it go on for?
Robert:	Till nine o'clock at night.
Arthur:	What about lunch?
Robert:	Half an hour.
Arthur:	Aren't there any breaks?
Robert:	Breaks? Oh yes –
Chorus:	– breaks in the machine when the wood gives way
	– breaks in bones when the frame comes down
	– breaks in the skin when the whip hits your back
Robert:	I broke the end off my finger. They wrapped it in cloth and made me go on working.
Arthur:	But what are you whipped for?
Chorus:	– working too slowly
	– working too fast
	– fighting and brawling

	– using ill-language
	– throwing water at Ann Gregory
	– striking T. Ride on the nose
	– stealing or eating
	– larking or breathing

Robert: Fun. That's why I'm running away.

Arthur: I see. (*A brief pause*) Where will you go, then?

Robert: London, I suppose.

Arthur: But what'll you do?

Robert: I'll be an apprentice to someone – but I'm not going back to Litton mill.

Jenks (*entering*): Here he is, Sam. We've got him. (*Sam enters*) Come on, Mr. Blincowe, time to go home.

Arthur: You're not to take him. (*Jenks and Sam ignore Arthur and grab Robert. He struggles, and Arthur joins in Sam grabs at Arthur.*)

Sam: Right, you young scamp, you're coming as well.

Robert: Get off my hand, you're breaking my hand! (*All four scuffle as Adam enters.*)

Arthur: Father!

Mr. Slaney: Let go of him, mister, or I'll break your neck.

Sam: All right, all right. You can have that one. I don't want him anyway.

Arthur: Father, don't let them. They're taking Robert –

Mr. Slaney: Robert who?

Jenks: Robert Blincowe, sir. Here (*to Sam; Sam hands over certificate. Jenks reads*) – 'Apprenticed to our master, Mr. Ellis Needham, of Litton Mill.' It's all legal, as you can see. You can read, I take it?

Mr. Slaney: Er . . . ay . . . well, if it's legal . . .

Arthur: But they're taking him back to the mill.

Jenks: That's right, where he belongs. Come on. (*Jenks and Sam exit, dragging Robert with them. Adam and Arthur watch.*)

Arthur: Father, stop them!

Mr. Slaney: We can't help it, Arthur. It's nowt to do wi'us.

Song We are not Greek philosophers
Who live in Belper town,
We like to take a look at folk
Sort of sniff them up and down;
You might think we're insensitive
Though we'd gladly stop a crime,
But when moral questions complicate
We like to take our time.
There are lots of problems in the world,

Lots of people make a fuss,
There are places we don't know about
But it isn't up to us.
So you see we couldn't interfere,
Men have got to earn their pay,
If another feller does his job
We look the other way.

Scene Four

The Slaney cottage. Mrs. Slaney is sewing, Ellen cooking and Grandmother is seated. Jem enters, dripping, and throws down his spade.

Jem:	Phew!
Ellen:	Who threw you in the brook, then?
Mrs. Slaney:	Now don't tease the lad. You can see he's tired.
Jem:	Tired? I'm aching all over. I thought digging coal was hard work, but it's nothing to digging the cut. Standing there up to your waist in water, digging away.
Ellen:	Nobody asked you to, did they?
Jem:	Didn't they, though? Mr. Strutt gives two shillings a day and free ale, and you can't get asked better than that.
	(*Will and Arthur enter.*)
Will:	I thought you didn't like Mr. Strutt.
Jem:	I don't want to work in his mill, but I don't mind drinking his ale.
Mrs. Slaney:	Anything for beer and money, eh Jem?
Jem:	Anything but work inside, mother.
Will:	But what'll you do when the channel's done? Strutt'll still want men to work at the mill.
Jem:	Not me, Will. I'm off to Pentrich. Mr. Hunt wants an apprentice labourer.
Ellen:	But he's only a farmer.
Jem:	That'll do for me.
Will:	Mr. George Strutt is likely to take over his father's mill. Seems to me he's more likely to encourage a young lad. Eh, Jem?
Jem:	Maybe, Will, but it's not for me.
Arthur:	I hate the mill. You mustn't work there.
Mrs. Slaney:	You know nothing about it, young Arthur.
Grandmother:	What's all the fuss about?

Ellen:	Oh, Grandmother, how can you? Haven't you seen the new mill?
Grandmother:	No, and I don't want to.
Ellen:	It's marvellous. A huge great hall – it's as large as Lincoln Cathedral.
Grandmother:	Don't tell me stories. Just 'cos it's new.
Arthur:	It's horrible. Like a big prison.
Mrs. Slaney:	You've not worked there, young Arthur, so you don't know.
Ellen:	Well, they're starting a new school there, so you'll have a chance to find out.
Arthur:	I'm not going.
Jem:	I am. I'm off to Pentrich, to see Mr. Hunt. (*To Susan*) Tell my father, will you?
Mr. Slaney	(*entering from nailshop*): Tell your father what?
Jem:	I'm going to Hunt's at Pentrich. An apprentice.
Mr. Slaney:	Apprentice – to a farmer? What sort of life do you call that?
Mrs. Slaney:	It's what he wants, Adam.
Mr. Slaney:	It may be what he wants, but it's not what I want. There's Will here can't stop talking about the mill, you going off to God knows where.
Jem:	At least I'll be my own man.
Will:	And what d'you mean by that?
Jem:	I'll get my full wages.
Will:	So will I.
Jem:	That's not what I hear. One sixth of your wages at the mill are stopped, they say, in case you get into trouble.
Mr. Slaney:	How d'you mean, trouble?
Jem:	Drinking, fighting, swearing.
Will:	Ah, but if you don't get into trouble you get your money.
Jem:	Every three months you do.
Mr. Slaney:	Well, that's not right.
Mrs. Slaney:	It is, too. There's enough brawling goes on around here, and if Mr. Strutt can stop it, good luck to him.
Jem:	Good luck to me, too. I'm off.
Mrs. Slaney:	Take care, lad.
Jem:	Don't worry, mother, I'll be back (*Exit*).
Mr. Slaney:	So that's one gone.
Will:	I'm still going to the mill, father.
Mr. Slaney:	If you must, you must, but you're daft.
Will:	They all said that at first, but look how many's at the mill now.
Grandmother:	All these folks, doing nothing but make cloth. It don't seem right.
Mrs. Slaney:	You'll be glad enough to wear it when winter's in.

Will:	It's different, father, things are changing. They said the machines couldn't work, and the mill would never get men, but they were wrong. George Strutt's the man.
Ellen:	He's handsome, too. (*Arthur mimes kisses at her.*) And I don't know what you're being so silly for. If it weren't for him you wouldn't have the chance of going to school.
Arthur:	I don't want to go to his school, and I don't want to work in the mill.
Will:	You don't know what it's like.
Arthur:	I know what Litton mill's like.
Will:	Litton? That's the worst in the country. Strutt's mill won't be like that.
Arthur:	How do you know?
Ellen:	And if you're not going to work in the mill you'll need some education to get you a better job, so you can go to the school and like it.

Song	The urge for independence grows, All creatures need to roam, A boy who wants to be a man Can't spend his life at home; They've reared you and they've loved you But deep down inside you know No matter what the old folks say The time has come to go: No matter if they weep and cry It's your chance if you dare Look up above you to the sky – There's changes in the air.

Scene Five

A small room at the Pentrich Inn. Isaac Ludlam is seated at a table, reading. He closes his book as Jeremiah Brandreth and Samuel Hunt enter.

Ludlam:	Good-day, Jeremiah, Samuel.
Brandreth:	And to you, Isaac.
Ludlam:	How goes it?
Hunt:	They're angry, and I don't blame them. There's fourteen acres of common land just vanished. Squire's put up fences, and there's dogs and keepers all over.

50

Ludlam:	I know. I've just come from Simon Parkin's house. His lad was shot in the leg last night, and even if the constables don't find him he'll not walk properly again.
Brandreth:	Poor lad.
Oliver	(*entering*): Good evening, gentlemen. I've not kept you waiting, I trust?
Ludlam:	Not long, Oliver.
Oliver:	Good. Well?
Ludlam:	You've heard about the Parkins' boy?
Oliver:	Indeed. A sad case – but good for the cause. Our people are angry, are they not? Such incidents breed discontent with the government, which we must welcome.
Hunt:	That's true.
Ludlam:	But how much discontent? Are we enough?
Oliver:	Ah, now there I think I can help you. I have come this very day from Manchester and before that from Leeds. All over the north our allies are preparing to march on London.
Brandreth:	That's good news, but when?
Oliver:	Very soon, my friends, very soon.
Ludlam:	We shall be accused of treason, of aiding the French.
Oliver:	We shall be accused of many things, my good friend, but our cause is just, is it not?
Hunt:	Why, we ask only for freedom before the law, bread to eat, equality between men.
Oliver:	Quite so, quite so.
Brandreth:	Besides, if we're strong enough no one'll accuse us of anything. It'll be our place to accuse, and there's plenty we'll find guilty.
Oliver:	Well said, brother Jeremiah, well said.
Ludlam:	What, then, are our plans?
Oliver:	Gather, on Friday next, with as many men as you can muster, here in Pentrich. From here, at about six in the evening, you should march towards Nottingham. Others will join you from all parts – Sheffield, Manchester, Leeds.
Ludlam:	One moment. You speak as if you will not be with us.
Oliver:	I? Oh, I promise you, I shall be with you – in spirit at least. It may be, however, that our friends elsewhere will have more urgent need of me.
Brandreth:	We'll march if there's only the three of us.
Oliver:	Brave words, Jeremiah, brave words. Rest assured, if I cannot be with you at the start of the march, I shall be with you – in spirit at least. It may be, however, that our friends elsewhere will have more urgent need of me.

Brandreth:	We'll march if there's only the three of us.
Oliver:	Brave words, Jeremiah, brave words. Rest assured, if I cannot be with you at the start of the march, I shall eagerly await you in Nottingham.
Jem	(*entering*): Pardon, Mister Hunt, but the barley is done. Shall I go down to the brook?
Hunt:	Ay, Jem, that'll be fine. I'll not be long. (*Jem goes out.*)
Brandreth:	He looks a promising lad. Strong, is he?
Hunt:	Jem? Good worker, Belper lad, just come this week.
Oliver:	Belper, eh? And who do we have in Belper?
Ludlam:	Ephraim Ward, and a handful of others.
Brandreth:	Most of 'em are in Strutts' mill. They won't fight.
Oliver:	Well, enlist young Jem if you can. He should be useful. Good-day. (*Oliver goes.*)

Song	You humble, simple working men,
	Why won't you understand?
	The masters that you labour for
	It's them that stole your land;

They say you owe them your respect,
They say you must obey
But every time you bow your head
They're taking more away;
Don't listen to the gentry's lie
But fight to keep your share
The fire of justice burns the sky
There's changes in the air.

Scene Six

Darkness, broken by the growing sight and sound of fire. Only as the scene develops do we realise that it takes place in the Slaney cottage, at night.

Will:	It's burning, father, get up. The mill's burning – look down in the valley.
Mr. Slaney:	All right, then, come on. Susan!
Mrs. Slaney:	What is it?
Grandmother:	What's the matter?
Ellen:	What's happening?
Mr. Slaney:	Get some broth on, we'll need it when we get back.
Mrs. Slaney:	Where are you going?
Will:	The mill's burning, mother.
Grandmother:	If it's burning it's burning – you'll not stop it now.

Will: Well, we'll try. Come on father. (*Will and Mr. Slaney exit.*)

Mrs. Slaney: I've never seen Will care for anything like the mill.

Ellen: It's Mr. Strutt that's done it. He gets things done. And he thinks highly of our Will, too.

Grandmother: He'll not think highly of anyone if his mill's burnt to the ground.

Mrs. Slaney: You don't know it'll burn that quickly.

Ellen: You've not seen it, mother. The frames are all wood, and there's great oak beams from one end of the hall to the other. There's thread, and cloth, and oil – once a fire starts there's no knowing what it'll do.

Grandmother: I reckon that's the last we'll see of grand young Mr. Strutt and his city ways.

Mrs. Slaney: Don't say that, mother, you know how Will thinks of him.

Grandmother: I know how our Ellen thinks of him.

Ellen: Don't be silly, Grandmother, you know I've no interest in Mr. Strutt. Not really, that is. But it'd be a shame if the mill burnt down.

Grandmother: Make no great difference.

Mrs. Slaney: How can you say such a thing, with your own family doing so well out of it?

Ellen: What I want to know is, how did the fire start?

Mrs. Slaney: What d'you mean?

Ellen: Well, they say there's spinners from Lancashire going round smashing looms and burning the mills, because the new machines have put men out of work.

Grandmother: That's right.

Mrs. Slaney: Ellen, don't say such a thing.

Ellen: But that's what they say, mother. And you know yourself there's folk round here desperate enough to do it.

Mrs. Slaney: There's folk round here desperate enough to do owt.

Grandmother: Young Ephraim Ward keeps telling 'em – someone'll pay, he says, someone'll pay for all the suffering soon enough.

Mrs. Slaney: But you know what a fool Ephraim is.

Ellen: There's more than him. There's people that have lost their jobs to the machines and can't afford food – why, Jem said only the other day about folk at Pentrich losing their land.

Mrs. Slaney: Ay, but they'll not have burnt the mill.

Ellen: Maybe they have and maybe they haven't, but it's worth thinking about.

Mrs. Slaney: I don't like to think about it, just when things were going so well. (*Mr. Slaney and Will return.*) Well, son, how was it?

Will:	Burnt to the ground. There's nothing left.
Grandmother:	Didn't I tell you?
Mr. Slaney:	There was nowt we could do.
Ellen:	I'm sorry, Will.
Will:	It's all right, though. It's going to be all right.
Ellen:	How d'you mean?
Will:	Mr. Strutt was there, he watched his mill burn down. And d'you know what, mother, you'll never guess what he said.
Mrs. Slaney:	I can't think. There's not much to say.
Will:	As soon as he knew there was no hope, he stands up where everyone can see him and says, 'Right, we'll build another mill.'
Mr. Slaney:	That's right.
Will:	And we'll keep our jobs and there'll be a new mill built in no time.
Mrs. Slaney:	Oh, that's good, Will. I am glad.
Will:	He's a great man, is Mr. Strutt, a great man.

The dream of progress cannot die
The vision lingers there
The smoke still spirals through the sky
There's changes in the air.

Scene Seven

The Angel, Belper. Arnold, behind the bar, is talking with Richard Miller and John Watson.

Richard:	Mind you, I'll say this for him. He knows what he wants.
John:	And he takes it, too.
Arnold:	Not just for himself, though. There's a lot more come in here since the mills have opened.
John:	But it's not like it was, eh?
Arnold:	Bit quieter, but we do all right.
Richard:	Roads are better, too. Roads that Strutt's done are a sight better than the old 'uns was.
John:	Ah – remember old Bill Blount? Used to dig up the road to get his coal.
Arnold:	He'd not manage that too often with the wagons they get leaving the mill. I've never seen so many.
Richard:	He's changed Belper, no question of it.
	(*Will and Mr. Slaney enter.*)
John:	Afternoon Adam, Will. Early for you, isn't it?

Mr. Slaney:	We're celebrating, John. Young Will here's just been made overseer.
Richard:	Well done, lad.
John:	At the mill, is that?
Will:	That's right, Mr. Watson.
John:	Now then, young Will, you didn't talk like that when you kicked my shins in that Saint Monday.
Arnold:	He's respectable gentry now, John, gone up in the world.
Mr. Slaney:	Married, too.
John:	Well, I never. I'm getting old afore I know it. All the best, lad. Where will you be living?
Will:	We've got one of the new mill cottages.
Arnold:	Is that what they call Long Row?
Will:	That's it.
John:	Them poky little stalls on top of each other with no room for a nailshop?
Arnold:	Hush, John, it's the lad's first home.
Will:	That's alright, Arnold, I know what I'm getting. They're strongly built and near the mill – for three shillings a week.
Richard:	And is it right you get cheap food from the mill?
Will:	That's right.
Richard:	So you'll know where to go if things get hard, eh, Adam?
Mr. Slaney:	I'll manage without that.
Will:	But you know it's there if you need it.
Arnold:	And that's all for three shillings a week?
Will:	That's it – as long as you keep it clean.
Arnold:	But they're not to know, eh?
Will:	Oh, they send round inspectors to look after the building, and they clean the chimneys four times a year.
John:	No, no. You're not your own man – not if they're selling you food and walking in and out of your house.
Will:	I'm not complaining.
John:	But that's no kind of a life.
Richard:	You stop there, John Watson. It's not your life we're talking about, but young Will's, so let's stop moaning, eh?
Mr. Slaney:	Well said, Richard. Come on then, Arnold, we'll have a glass all round. Where's Ephraim?
Arnold:	He's not been in for some days.
Richard:	Very strange, he was. 'Bout a week ago, started muttering about changes, and we'd talk to him differently in a couple of months.
John:	Now, what I fancy is that he's gone to Lancashire, looking for the rebels.

Richard:	Looking for trouble, more like.
Mr. Slaney:	What do they reckon to do, then?
Richard:	Oh, they want cheaper bread, and the land that the squires took.
Arnold:	Seems fair enough.
Richard:	Maybe, but they'll not get it.
John:	Not unless they fight for it, you mean.
Richard:	I can't see Ephraim doing much fighting. He was never much use in a brawl.
Mr. Slaney:	He'd have been all right if he'd have been half sober.
Richard:	Well, they may be having a hard time of it in the north, but we're all right here, eh?
Mr. Slaney:	Ay, I had my worries when they built the first mill, but it's turned out for the best.
Arnold:	Right, then, Will. What'll it be?
Will:	Here's to advancement – and progress. (*Drinks*)
All:	Advancement – and progress (*All drink*).

Scene Eight

An empty classroom at the Strutt's mill school. Very neat and orderly. A handbell rings outside, and the children walk in and sit down. Ellen, as a pupil teacher, enters.

Ellen:	Good morning, girls.
All:	Good morning, Miss Slaney.
Ellen:	Miss Price has asked me to continue with your lesson, as she has a very important visitor. (*Jane raises hand.*) Yes, Jane?
Jane:	It's Mr. George Strutt. We saw him arrive. He looks ever so well.
Mary:	Jane's in love with him.
Jane:	I'm not.
Jill:	Do you like Mr. Strutt, Miss Slaney?
Ellen:	He's a very fine man, he's done a lot for the town. But that's enough idle chatter for today; we have our work to do. Nancy, read from Genesis, chapter one, verse thirty one, if you please.
Nancy:	'And God saw everything that he had made, and behold, it was very good.'
Ellen:	Thankyou. Genesis teaches us that God made all things and we should praise him for it. Jill, read through the verses you have written and tell me one of our Lord's creations.

Jill:	He made the land and the sea, Miss Slaney.
Ellen:	Good. Jane, can you tell me what else was created?
Jane:	The sun and the stars, Miss Slaney.
Ellen:	Sally? What did our Lord create? (*Sally nervous, says nothing.*) What did he create? What did he make?
Sally:	The mm . . . mm . . . mm . . . mill? (*Giggles from the others.*)
Jill:	Why are they laughing, Miss Slaney? Didn't God make the mill?
Mary:	Don't be silly. Mr. Strutt made the mill.
Jill:	Didn't God make it, then?
Nancy:	Mr. Strutt isn't God.
Betty:	My uncle Ephraim says he's the devil. (*Shocked reaction.*)
Ellen:	Betty! Now, girls, Miss Price will return soon and she will want to know what you have learnt from Genesis. She will not want to hear what Ephraim Ward has to say. Now, continue your copying with Chapter Two. (*Girls read and write in silence.*)
	(*Miss Price enters, and the girls rise instantly.*)
Miss Price:	Thank you, girls, you may sit down. What are you reading, Mary?
Mary:	The book of Genesis, the second chapter, Miss Price.
Miss Price:	Very well, continue. (*The girls continue to work in silence while Miss Price talks confidentially to Ellen.*) Have they worked well?
Ellen:	Oh yes, Miss Price.
Miss Price:	You enjoy teaching them? Good. Now, I have good news. Mr. Strutt is to hold a celebration.
Ellen:	Mr. George Strutt?
Miss Price:	He was my visitor. He invites us to dine with him on Friday.
Ellen:	To dine, with him? But . . . who is invited?
Miss Price:	All who work at the mill, or who attend his school. It will be a fine occasion.
Ellen:	He has done well for Belper.
Miss Price:	He has done well for himself. He is also engaged to be married. Now, girls, I have good news for you. Mr. Strutt has awarded you all a half-day holiday (*mild excitement and chatter, which stops as soon as Miss Price continues*) and also invites you and your families to the Hall, for a celebration this very Friday (*cheers*). Now, let us pray. (*All the girls bow their heads, although Betty looks up and around the room as the prayer goes on.*) We pray for our King and his ministers, that they may guide us in the paths of righteousness. And we give thanks for our founder and benefactor

Mister George Strutt, who has given us this school and brought prosperity to our town. Amen.

(*All the girls say Amen, except Betty. Jane is obviously louder than the others.*) Stand. (*Girls stand.*) Dismiss. (*Girls go out, in a very orderly way.*)

Miss Price: Young Jane always seems to pray harder where Mister Strutt is concerned. I fear she may be disappointed.

Ellen: Jane will learn. Mr. Strutt's in a different world from us.

Miss Price: Not so far away as that. He thinks highly of your brother Will, and if you continue to work as you have done you'll certainly improve yourself. Or perhaps you already have hopes of your own?

Ellen: Oh no, Miss Price. My hope is to be a teacher, like yourself.

Miss Price: Well, we shall see. The girls work well for you, and I shall happily recommend you. In fact, Mr. Strutt has asked if the girls from the school might supply some entertainment for the dinner. Perhaps you might teach them a dance?

Ellen: If you wish, Miss Price.

Miss Price: Yes, that would be most fitting. Mr. Strutt's young lady shall be introduced to the accomplishments of our young ladies. That will do very well, do you not think?

Ellen: Oh yes, Miss Price.

(*Miss Price goes out, leaving Ellen alone.*)

Song   You're born in a world that they never explain,
It gives you a promise, then cheats you again,
You're dimly aware things are not what they seem
But when you're a child you still have to dream.

Whatever you dream can be better than real
Although words cannot say all the feelings you feel.
You know when the day breaks the vision has gone,
You look out the window and life must go on.

You work in the daytime, you laugh if you can;
You love if you're lucky but worship no man,
Your common sense tells you things are what they seem
But if you're alive then you still have to dream.

Scene Nine

In a street outside a tavern in Codnor, on the Nottingham road. A crowd of marchers gather, singing the revolution song.

Every man his skill must try
He must turn out and not deny
No bloody soldiers must we dread
We must turn out and fight for bread
The time is come you plain must see
The Government opposed must be.

Three strangers approach.

Hunt:	Well, sir, will you join us?
First Stranger:	What are you for?
Ludlam:	Cheaper bread, freedom, the return of common land.
Second Stranger:	I'll join yer.
Third Stranger:	Where are you marching?
Brandreth:	Nottingham.
Third Stranger:	My master won't let me.
Brandreth	(*more threatening*): We said, will ye join us?
Third Stranger:	Ay, I'll join, I'll join.
Arthur	(*running in*): Jem, Jem!
Jem:	What are you doing in Codnor?
Arthur:	I heard they were marching. I knew you'd be here.
Jem:	But your mother and father . . .
Arthur:	They don't know. Let me stay, please, Jem.
Jem:	It'll be dangerous when we reach Nottingham. They'll have the troops out there.
Arthur:	I know. I want to come. Please.
Jem:	We'll see. Keep close.
Arthur:	Who's the leader?
Jem:	Oliver. But he's not here. So there's Mister Brandreth – that's him – and the Reverend Ludlam. He's a good man.
Arthur:	But how can Oliver be the leader if he's not here?
Jem:	It's difficult. We're not sure what's happening. Mister Hunt, is Mister Oliver here yet?
Hunt:	Not yet, Jem, not yet, but we'll see him in Nottingham. This may be news now.
Ephraim	(*entering, triumphant*): Victory! Victory! The troops at Nottingham have mutinied, we've won! (*wild cheers.*)
Arthur:	But Jem, it's Ephraim.
Jem:	I know. I don't like this.
Arthur:	How far is it to Nottingham, Jem?

Jem:	Ten miles or more yet. Mister Brandreth, do we know that's right?
Ephraim:	Are you calling me a liar, Jem Slaney?
Jem:	No, Ephraim, but did you see the soldiers?
Ephraim:	One of the King's own troopers rode up to me and told me. Ride post haste, he said, and tell the Pentrich men that we'll fight for them against the King (*cheers*).
Ludlam:	Let's press on, Jeremiah.
	(*Protest from marchers – 'No . . . we've got a victory to celebrate . . . let's have some ale . . .' and so on.*)
Brandreth:	Victory is ours, Mister Ludlam. We could take a glass of ale and claim Nottingham at our leisure. (*Loud cheers of approval, as the marchers go into the tavern.*)
Jem:	But if it's a trick . . .
Brandreth:	Jem, we'll take a glass of ale. (*Ludlam, Hunt and Brandreth go into the tavern.*)
Jem:	Arthur, you're not to stay.
Arthur:	But if we've won?
Jem:	We may not have. You're to go back to your mother and tell her what you've seen. You'll hear the news of what happens soon enough.
Arthur:	But what about you, Jem?
Jem:	I've said I'll stay.
Arthur:	Can't I stay with you?
Jem:	No. I've told you – now go home. If we take Nottingham, you can join us for the march on London.
Arthur:	Oh please, Jem, send for me.
Jem:	I promise. Now, go home.
Arthur:	Good luck, Jem. (*Arthur runs off. Jem watches him go and then slowly follows Brandreth Hunt and Ludlam into the tavern.*)

Scene Ten

The same Friday evening, in the Slaney cottage, with the family preparing to go to the Strutt dinner.

Song   Life isn't what you asked for but
You do the best you can,
The luxury of freedom doesn't
Suit a working man;
We're some way short of paradise
But all men's dreams must fail,
Before the darkness closes in
We'll drink a glass of ale.

Ellen:	Do I look all right, mother?
Mrs. Slaney:	Of course you do, Ellen.
Ellen:	Do you think the dance will go well?
Mrs. Slaney:	If worrying could help, it'd be perfect. Now go and have another look for Arthur and your father. Come on, mother, get ready.
Grandmother:	What's all the fuss for?
Mrs. Slaney:	You know very well what the fuss is for. Mister Strutt's giving us all a feast, with the war over and the mill making money again.
Grandmother:	Load of nonsense, if you ask me.
Mrs. Slaney:	You'd have said more than that if Napoleon had landed on your doorstep. (*Adam comes in, breathless and gloomy.*) Well, and about time.
Mr. Slaney:	Now you hold your tongue till you've heard me speak. There's trouble ahead.
Grandmother:	What trouble?
Mr. Slaney:	Richard Miller says there's been riots, men marching on Nottingham. The way he tells it, there's been troops out.
Grandmother:	I've told you, you can't deny that. You can't take folks' land and livelihood away without there's trouble.
Mrs. Slaney:	Don't go on, now, mother –
Ellen:	Besides, I don't see what it's got to do with us.
Mr. Slaney:	Well you're not as clever as I take you for, then. There's men from Pentrich been marching, Richard says, and if Pentrich farmers are marching then our Jem'll be there.
Ellen:	Not if he's any sense.
Mrs. Slaney:	Jem's sense enough to do what's right.
Mr. Slaney:	Ay, but what's right? Jem's a powerful sense of how things ought to be, but there's no saying all men'll take his part.
Ellen:	He should have gone to the mill.
Grandmother:	He'd not have lasted a day. He's his own man, is Jem. He's better where he is.
Mrs. Slaney:	And where's that, then? (*Knock on door. They wait, nervously.*) Adam, who is it?
Mr. Slaney:	How should I know, woman? Open the door, go on. (*She does.*)
Ephraim	(*entering, sheepish*): Ah, Susan Slaney, you're my saviour.
Mr. Slaney:	Drinking again then, Ephraim?
Ephraim:	I'm drunk, Adam, I swear it – drunk with fear – and that's all.
Ellen:	But you're surely not a man that's frightened, Mr. Ward?

Ephraim:	That's not fair, Miss Ellen, to mock a man in a desperate plight. Soldiers, Adam. They've sent soldiers after us, with swords and rifles.
Mr. Slaney:	Where were you?
Ephraim:	Codnor way. Going for Nottingham, we were, and they sent an army against us.
Grandmother:	And you ran like chickens, eh?
Ephraim:	I'll fight with any man fair and square, but even Ephraim Ward doesn't stand to be ridden down by troopers. Two hundred of them there were – or maybe five hundred.
Mrs. Slaney:	What of our Jem, then?
Ephraim:	Called me a liar, he did. I warned him, told him the troops were after us, and he called me a liar.
Mr. Slaney:	Well you are a liar, Ephraim, and you know it. Richard Miller hears there were fifty soldiers at most, so where's your five hundred got to? (*Pause.*) Did you see Jem when the soldiers came?
Ephraim:	When the soldiers came, Adam, I saw nothing. A man looks after his skin and no more. I saw him at Codnor, though, and Arthur.
Mrs. Slaney:	Arthur, at Codnor? If this is one of your stories, Ephraim Ward –
Ephraim:	As sure as I stand here.
Mrs. Slaney:	God help us, what'll happen to the lad?
Ellen:	He's a fool, mother.
Mrs. Slaney:	That's as maybe, but I'd still wish him safe.
Ellen:	Mother, it's the feast. We must go now, or we'll be late.
Ephraim:	Feast? What feast is that?
Mr. Slaney:	Strutt's giving a dinner for all who work at the mill.
Ephraim:	Huh. You'll not see me there, then.
Grandmother:	You're not invited.
Ephraim:	And if I were, I'd not take so much as a chicken bone from Strutt. Now a glass of ale, mind . . .
Mr. Slaney:	Ephraim, you'll not stay here when we've gone.
Ephraim:	I'd thought, Adam, till the soldiers went . . .
Ellen:	And we're to go to prison for your folly?
Ephraim:	But your Jem –
Ellen:	I'll not answer for him. It's him that chooses to take the risk of hanging.
Mrs. Slaney:	Ellen, there's no sense in such talk.
Ellen:	And there's no sense in any talk here. I'm going, mother; shall I go alone? (*Standing up.*)
Mr. Slaney:	No, we'll come. Go on, Ephraim, out with you. (*Softer*) Hide in the barn if you must. (*To Grandmother*) Come on then, mother. (*Ephraim goes slowly out, family prepare to leave.*)

Mrs. Slaney:	But what about Arthur?
Mr. Slaney:	Ay. Well, he may come and he may not. There's little we can do.
Mrs. Slaney:	I'll wait, Adam. He may come.
Mr. Slaney:	As you will. Come then, mother, Ellen. We'll see your girls dance yet. (*They go off, leaving Mrs. Slaney sewing slowly. Sudden noise outside as Arthur stumbles in, exhausted.*)
Mrs. Slaney:	Arthur!
Arthur:	Mother . . . Are the soldiers here?
Mrs. Slaney:	No, love, you're safe. Where have you been?
Arthur:	With Jem at Codnor.
Mrs. Slaney:	You've walked, from Codnor?
Arthur:	Run, mother. Jem sent me home and I'd not gone half a mile when there was shooting and screaming, soldiers riding past and . . . then there was nothing.
Mrs. Slaney:	There, lad, you're safe now.
Arthur:	But what about Jem?
Mrs. Slaney:	We'll know soon enough. They may tell us at the feast. Shall we go now?
Arthur:	I'm not going to Strutt's feast.
Mrs. Slaney:	But Arthur – there's Ellen's girls dancing, and Will done so well, and –
Arthur:	And Jem?
Mrs. Slaney:	Mister Strutt's not to blame for Jem, son.
Arthur:	I'll not go.
Mrs. Slaney:	You'll not help Jem by crying at home. (*Arthur stays silent, seated.*) Arthur, love, if Jem's caught then Mister Strutt may speak for him. We can ask Will if he'll . . .
Arthur:	No! I'll not go mother, never.
	(*Slow fade down, with both characters still.*)
Song	You live and work as best you can You take what life will give, You take some knocks you can't avoid And some you can't forgive; You know you can't do more than hope You settle for what's there, You can't be sure what lies ahead There's changes in the air.

See How You Go

Clare Holden
Mrs. Prentiss – *Clare's supervisor*
Alison – *a typist*
Shelley – *branch organiser of a union*
Mr. Neale – *Clare's boss*

Mr. Morley – *managing director*
Mr. Len Holden – *Clare's father*
Mrs. Sheila Holden – *his wife*
Mick, *their son*
Grandfather

The play takes place in a small Midlands town. The time is the present.

Scene One

Just before 9.00 am at Carlton's, a large firm. During the scene the action moves between two areas, an office used by a group of typists, and Mr. Neale's personal office, which is smaller but more luxurious. If possible, both should be visible all the time, and the movement between the two should be managed through lighting, as smoothly and quickly as possible.

(A) In the typists' office, Mrs. Prentiss is busy, tidying papers efficiently. Alison comes in and hangs up her coat.

Alison:	Morning, Mrs. P.
Mrs. P.:	Hello, Alison. Have a nice weekend?
Alison:	Oh yes. Went to a great concert on Saturday.
Mrs. P.:	Not my sort of concert, I suppose.
Alison:	It might be. You don't know till you try.
Mrs. P.:	I don't think so.
	(*Shelley comes in, a bit breathless.*)
Shelly:	Morning, Alison. Morning, Mrs. Prentiss.
Mrs. P.:	Good morning.

Alison:	Hi, Shelley. Have a good time?
Shelley:	Too good. I'd rather have stayed in bed than clock in here.
Mrs. P.:	Well, it's Monday morning and you can't change that.
Shelley:	I wouldn't mind trying.
Mrs. P.:	Anything to get out of work.
Alison:	Now, now, Mrs. P., we haven't started yet.
	(*Clare looks in, a bit nervously.*)
Mrs. P.:	Can I help you?
Clare:	I'm Clare Holden. I'm starting here today.
Mrs. P.:	Come in, love. Have you seen Mr. Neale?
Clare:	Not today. I saw him when I came for my interview. He said to come to the third floor and ask for Mrs. Prentiss.
Mrs. P.:	That's me.
Shelley:	You're going to work here, then?
Clare:	Well, I'd like to.
Shelley:	Are you in the union?
Mrs. P.:	Give her a chance, she's hardly got here.
Shelley:	I'm giving her a chance – a chance to join.
Mrs. P.:	Clare's only on a month's trial to start with. There'll be time enough for joining the union if she's given a permanent job. Have you done typing and shorthand?
Clare:	Yes, but only at college. This is my first job.
Shelley:	Well, you've chosen a good place to start. Mrs. P.'ll look after you, so long as you work twenty-four hours a day and don't stop to blow your nose.
Mrs. P.:	That's quite enough of that.
Shelley:	All right, Mrs. P., you know I'm joking.
Mrs. P.:	I'm never sure when you're serious, that's the trouble.
Alison:	You've been before, though, to your interview?
Clare:	Yes, with Mr. Neale. He seemed very nice.
Shelley:	Oh, Neale's all right. It's Morley you've got to watch.
Mrs. P.:	Don't be rude about Mr. Morley. He works very hard.
Shelley:	He works us hard, I know that. I'm not sure why they moved him in above Neale, but I know who I'd rather have.
	(*Neale comes in cheerily.*)
Neale:	Good morning, Mrs. Prentiss, Good morning, girls. Shelley, could I have a word in my office in a minute? Oh yes, . . . Clare Holden, isn't it?
Clare:	Yes, that's right.
Neale:	You found your way here all right, then?
Clare:	Yes, thankyou.
Neale:	Well, Mrs. Prentiss will take care of any problems. Just find your way around, and do your best. We'll give you a month and see how you go, all right?

Clare:	Yes. Thankyou, Mr. Neale.
Neale:	Right, I'll see you in a minute, then? (*Goes.*)
Shelley:	Righto, Mr. Neale. (*Looks in her bag*) Here, Clare, there's a union card. You can leave joining till you've got a permanent job if you like, but this'll tell you what it's about. I'll tell you about meetings over lunch. Must dash. (*Goes out.*)
Clare	(*A bit dazed*): Oh . . . er . . . right.
Alison:	There you are. It's as easy as that. Don't blink or you'll find you're a paid up member.
Mrs. P.:	I don't know why they bother.
Clare:	I don't really know anything about it . . .
Alison:	Don't worry. Just leave it to Shelley. She's a good organiser, and she'll let you know what's happening.
Mrs. P.:	All in good time, she will. First of all we'll get some work done – that is what we're here for, after all. Now, Clare, I'd like you to file these letters over here, clients in alphabetical order of surnames, most recent correspondence at the front of the file, and then there's some of Mr. Neale's correspondence . . .

(B) The scene fades to Mr. Neale's office, where Mr. Morley is in the middle of a brief visit.

Morley:	So it looks as though there'll have to be definite cutbacks on staffing.
Neale:	Finding people to retire early, you mean. That sort of thing.
Morley:	Well, I suppose that might help to begin with, but I'm looking for something rather more far-reaching.
Neale:	But we're doing so well –
Morley:	We're doing well because we're not throwing money away. I don't intend that we should start now. Competition will get tougher, not easier.
Neale:	I thought I ought to ask Miss Firth in, just to keep the union informed.
Morley:	Well, if you think it will do any good . . .
Neale:	But if you're thinking of redundancies we'll have to discuss it with them eventually.
Morley:	Oh yes, eventually. We'll go through the motions, and they'll make threatening noises.
Neale:	But this branch has always had a very good record for getting on with our workers –
Morley:	And a very bad one for economy. That is about to change. Anyway, we both know why I've been appointed here, so I needn't go over that again. (*Neale's phone rings, and he answers it, as Morley turns to go.*)

Neale:	Would you like to see Miss Firth?
Morley:	Not particularly.
Neale:	She is here now.
Morley:	Well, all right then. I suppose I might as well see how she takes it. Probably badly, knowing her.
	(*Knock on the door, and Shelley comes in, not noticing Mr. Morley straight away.*)
Shelley:	Morning, Mr. Neale.
Neale:	Hello, Shelley. Er, you know Mr. Morley?
Shelley:	Yes, of course. Good morning.
Morley:	Morning.
Neale:	Well . . . er . . . we've decided . . . I've called you in to give you some idea of what's in the pipeline.
Shelley:	Mass sackings and a cut in wages, is it?
Neale:	Now then, don't be naughty. No, it's just that, as you know, we're trying to break into the German market –
Shelley:	Yes?
Neale:	And in the short term . . .
Shelley:	How long's that?
Neale:	Well, the next few months, say.
Shelley:	Yes?
Neale:	We'll need to save as much money as we can, so that we're properly competitive . . .
Shelley:	You're not telling me anything new, Mr. Neale.
Morley:	Right. Let's be clear about this. We are on the edge of a breakthrough, a real explosion in sales, if we play our cards right. If we can persuade our German buyers that we can deliver on time and at the right price then in a year's time our trading position will look very healthy and your members can look forward to job security and some increase in pay.
Shelley:	But?
Morley:	But that has to be paid for. What we save on is surplus manpower, employees who don't give an economic return, wastage – you know the sort of thing.
Shelley:	You mean someone'll be out of a job?
Neale:	Well, I'm sure it needn't be as harsh as that . . .
Shelley:	Are you? I don't think Mr. Morley's sure of that.
Morley:	I'd rather not commit myself on the details. We'll have full guidelines from Head Office in a couple of days. We can discuss proposals then.
Shelley:	But they will take account of our negotiations last year?
Neale:	Oh yes, Shelley, there's no question that –
Morley:	This is a new situation, Mr. Neale. I'm sure Miss Firth's colleagues will see the long-term benefits this could bring them.

Shelley:	There's no long-term benefit in getting the sack.
Morley:	Well, I don't think there's any point in getting heated till we've some firm proposals to discuss. (*Gets up and leaves*) Good day.
Shelley:	Well, that looks pretty bad to me.
Neale:	I'm sure it'll turn out all right.
Shelley:	Well, I hope so, Mr. Neale, but I shouldn't like to bet on it.

(C) Back in the typists' office, later the same day. Alison is working at her desk while Mrs. Prentiss goes over Clare's work for the day.

Mrs. P.:	Well, this looks all right. That really ought to be a separate paragraph but it's not worth retyping specially, and it does look quite nice. It's good to see you can spell 'sincerely'.
Clare:	Thank you. (*Mrs. P. hands her work back, and goes out with a file.*)
Alison:	That was a dig at me. I spelt 'sincerely' wrong in one letter in my first week here and ever since Mrs. P's been sure that I'm part of a general decline in educational standards.
Clare:	She seems all right, though.
Alison:	Oh, she's fine. A bit old-fashioned, but she's not nasty, and she lets you get on with your work. There's some real dragons on the second floor.
Clare:	How does she get on with Shelley?
Alison:	Oh, all right really. They growl at each other a bit, but they're Ok most of the time. It's just the union. Mrs. P. hates the whole idea of unions, and Shelley's the branch organiser.
Clare:	She seems very keen.
Alison:	That's putting it mildly. 'Militant', Mrs. P. calls her. Anyway, I don't think they'll do each other any serious damage – it's just fun to watch the sparks fly now and again. How's your first day?
Clare:	Fine, I think. You never know what to expect before you start.
Alison:	I know. I remember my first day here. Scared stiff, I was, and then I got moaned at by Mr. Morley for typing an address wrong. I wanted to die.
Clare:	Well, I'm glad nothing like that's happened to me.
Alison:	Don't worry, it will.
Clare:	Well, thanks.
Alison:	Come on, don't just sit there. Time to go home.
Clare:	You mean we just pack up?
Alison:	Why not? Do you want to wait for the school bell?

Clare:	No, but it seems funny, just going.
Alison:	Well, Mrs. P. will be doing a few extra jobs. Just tidying up, she calls it. If she went home on time I think Carlton's would cave in.
Clare:	What about Shelley?
Alison:	Shelley? Five o'clock and that's it. She'll kill herself working for the union, but so far as the firm's concerned it's nine to five and not a second more.
Clare:	But where is she now?
Alison:	Some meeting, I shouldn't wonder. Still, don't let it worry you. That's why we elect her, to do the worrying for us. Come on. (*Alison goes and waits at the door, as Clare tidies up and collects her coat. They both go out.*)

Scene Two

Clare's home. A large kitchen where the family have their meals. The table is half set for tea, and there are odd magazines and bits of homework lying around. Mrs. Holden, Clare's mother, is busy making the tea while Mick reads a comic, sprawled on the floor.

Clare	(*entering*): Hello, mum, I'm back.
Mick:	That's a pity. We hoped you'd been run over.
Mrs. Holden:	Shut up, Mick. How was it, love?
Mick:	Haven't they sacked you yet?
Clare:	No, they haven't. It was all right. Quite easy, really. A few letters, some filing –
Mick	(*singing:*) 'When you're filing, when you're filing, the whole world . . .'
Clare:	What's got into you today?
Mick:	Maths exam. Two hours of steady torture. (*Silly voice*) It has been know to send people mad . . .
Clare:	That started long before you did maths.
Mick:	Right, you've asked for it. (*Slowly approaches, threatening.*)
Mrs. Holden:	That's enough, you two. Come on, Mick, tidy this stuff up before your dad comes in. Clare, tell your grandad we're ready, will you? (*Clare goes*) Come on, Mick, I said tidy it, not read it.
Mick:	Hang on a minute.
Mrs. Holden:	No I won't. We're having tea today, Monday, not next week. Just try to be a bit more considerate, and do stop teasing Clare.

Mick:	It's only a bit of fun, mum.
Mrs. Holden:	She's grown up now, you know, earning a living.
Mick	(*As Clare enters, with grandad. He moves slowly but is not a comic figure, and should not act like a caricature*): Well, she may be getting paid, but she doesn't look any older to me.
Clare:	Thanks a lot. Just watch and you'll see my grey hairs.
Grandad:	And what's wrong with grey hairs?
Clare:	Nothing, grandad. It's just Mick being silly.
Mick:	Don't worry. Just walk by and ignore me. Everyone else does.
Clare:	I wish I could.
Mrs. Holden:	You won't want any tea, then?
Mr. Holden	(*entering*): Tea? Did you say tea?
Mrs. Holden:	I've said little else for the last half hour.
Mr. Holden:	Well, why are we waiting, then? Don't hang about, I'm famished.
Mrs. Holden	(*irritated*): Do you know what it takes to have tea ready for five people the minute you choose to walk through the door?
Mr. Holden:	Yes, love, you.
Mrs. Holden:	Flattery'll get you anywhere, I suppose.
Mr. Holden:	Well, it should get me some tea, anyway. (*To Clare*) And how's the workers of the world?
Clare:	Working.
Mick:	Makes a change.
Clare:	Well, it's only for a month, to start with. Just to see how I get on.
Mr. Holden:	Ok, was it?
Clare:	Mmm. Quite nice, really. It's a big place, four floors, but our bit's all right, quite small really. Just four of us – a Mrs. Prentiss and a couple of other girls. I think they'll be Ok.
Mick:	What's the food like?
Clare:	Bit like school, really.
Mick	(*hands on his throat*): Aaagh, they got me! The dreaded cyanide gravy claims its fifteenth victim . . .
Mrs. Holden:	Mick, that'll do.
Clare:	No, it's just a big canteen. You go in and queue, not a bad choice. It tastes all right, it's just that there's so many people, and I don't know most of them.
Mrs. Holden:	And is that all?
Clare:	How d'you mean?
Mrs. Holden:	Your first day at work. Is that all that happened?
Clare:	What did you expect? Did you want me to rob the till, or get seduced by the managing director?
Mrs. Holden:	There's no need to be silly.

Clare:	I did talk about joining the union.
Mr. Holden:	I should hope so too. Eh, dad? (*He looks for agreement, and Grandad nods, thoughtfully.*)
Mrs. Holden:	Now you're not to go getting mixed up in any trouble, Clare.
Mr. Holden:	That's why she's right to join. To keep out of trouble. She's better off in than out.
Mrs. Holden:	But unions always seem to mean trouble nowadays.
Grandad:	Trouble for the bosses, you mean.
Mrs. Holden:	But the newspapers are full of it.
Grandad:	Bosses own the newspapers.
Mrs. Holden:	All right, there's no need to start all that again. It's all very well harking back to the bad old days, but things are different now. I mean, nobody's exactly starving, are they?
Mr. Holden:	There's plenty worse off than us, Sheila. It's not all like the adverts, you know.
Mick:	You going out on strike then, sis? Great. Everybody out! I'll come out in sympathy. No more homework.
Clare:	A big difference that'll make.
Mrs. Holden:	He's right, though, Len. That's all you ever hear about from the unions these days, strikes and trouble.
Mr. Holden:	That's just the papers and the telly. What do they know? If you're at work you've got to be with your mates. It stands to reason. I wouldn't want Clare to be any different.
Mrs. Holden:	I still wish she didn't have to join.
Clare:	I don't have to, mum. It's just that . . . well, everyone else is in it.
Mrs. Holden:	That's the point. Pressure. Forcing you to do what you don't want to do. Why should they tell you what to do?
Grandad:	Why should the bosses tell her what to do?
Mrs. Holden:	Because it's their business, dad. They own it. That Mr. Neale, who gave Clare the job in the first place, he sounded ever so nice. It won't get you in trouble, will it love?
Clare:	Don't be daft, mum. I've only got a card, that's all. I've not paid anything yet. It's not as if we were out on strike, you know.
Mrs. Holden:	Don't talk about it any more. You'll start your grandad off.
Mick:	Tick, tick, tick. Are you ready to explode, grandad?
Grandad:	You can laugh, young Mick, you don't remember. I was in the union, and proud of it. Now why should that be something to be ashamed of. You're talking as if it were a disease. 'Old grandad's goin' to have a fit cos we're talking about the union.'

Mrs. Holden:	Now I didn't mean that, dad –
Grandad:	I dunno what you meant, and I don't care. Now you listen, Clare. When I were seventeen we took over the works at Fawley; factories, warehouse, offices, the lot. The bosses were going to lock us out, but we got in and ran it ourselves before they had the chance. They tried to cut our wages, see, and they were going to sack the union secretary. Brian Hemsley. What a feller. Only five foot nothing, but he had more go than any man I've seen. Got killed in the war. Pilot, he was. Anyway, Brian organised it and it ran like clockwork. We were there a week and they couldn't get us out. Hoses, police, they tried everything. They sent Harold Makepeace a telegram saying his mother had died, but she hadn't. Just a trick, to get him out, but he didn't go. That was the union.
Mrs. Holden:	But that was years ago.
Grandad:	That's why they've got to be told. Lest we forget.
	(*Mick starts to play a mock violin, but Len gestures him to stop. A pause.*)
Clare:	But what were you fighting for, grandad?
Grandad:	The rights of the working man, Clare. The right of a man to his job, and a fair day's pay. Freedom to organise, to defend ourselves.
Clare:	But it's not like that now.
Grandad:	That's what we fought for, and it don't change.
Mr. Holden:	You're right there, dad.
Mrs. Holden:	Don't encourage him, Len.
Grandad:	The bosses are still there. They may be younger, or softer, or better educated, but they're still there and they're still bosses, living off the skill of their workers. We've always had to fight for everything we got, and to fight you've got to be together. United we stand, divided we fall.
Mick:	Hurray!
Clare:	But grandad, I've only got a card.
Grandad:	I don't know why you've got it, love, but that's why it's there, and don't you forget it.
Mrs. Holden:	Can we close this meeting now, and do some washing up?
Mr. Holden:	Come on, dad. Let's look at the news. Mick, give your mum a hand, will you? (*Mick pulls a face, as Len and Grandad go off to the front room.*)
Mrs. Holden:	Huh. Workers of the world unite.
Clare:	Don't worry, mum, I'll help.
Mrs. Holden:	But it's your first day, love.
Clare:	Don't fret. There'll be plenty more.

Scene Three

If possible, this scene should be performed with
Neale's office and the typing office both visible all
the time, although the main action moves between
them.

(A) Neale in his office. Morley comes in briskly.

Morley: Ah, Neale. The guidelines are through, and I don't
think you'll get a heart attack. They're very mild. Not
as drastic as I'd have liked, really.

Neale: Oh, that is a relief.

Morley: We're not to touch existing permanent staff, although
we shall cut down on part-timers, of course. There's a
scheme to help early retirement and a freeze on new
appointments.

Neale: So you don't think there'll be trouble?

Morley: No, not a whisper. Lots of fuss about nothing if you
ask me.

Neale: Oh, good. I must say, I was hoping there wouldn't be
trouble.

Morley: You can't always run away from it, you know.

Neale: Oh no, quite. Er, there was just one thing . . .

Morley: Yes?

Neale: The new girl, Clare Holden. In Mrs. Prentiss' depart-
ment.

Morley: What about her?

Neale: She's on a month's trial; due to finish next week.

Morley: Well?

Neale: She's doing quite well. It is all right to appoint her, I
suppose?

Morley: Of course not.

Neale: But why not?

Morley: Mr. Neale, there's little point in head office sending
orders if you're going to ignore them.

Neale: But one seventeen-year-old girl –

Morley: You don't save money by worrying about individuals.
There's a freeze – that means no new jobs. It's simple.

Neale: But I've told her we'll take her on if she fits in.

Morley: That's too bad. We can't employ her.

Neale: But . . . well, it does seem hard. When will you tell
her?

Morley: I shan't. You will. As soon as possible, I'd say. (*Goes
out.*)

(B) Switch back to the typing office, where Mrs. Prentiss is again going over some of Clare's work.

Mrs. P.:	Well, I must say, these are very good, Clare.
Clare:	Thank you. I do feel I'm getting the hang of it now.
Shelley	(*struggling with a difficult letter*): I wish I was.
Alison:	In no time at all you'll be in a groove like the rest of us, just ticking away.
Mrs. P.:	Well, if that's how you work I'm not surprised you make mistakes. Don't you pay any attention, Clare. Just keep going as you are and you can't go far wrong.
Clare:	Well, I'm not sure I'll be staying –
Alison:	What's the matter, gone off us already?
Clare:	No, it's not that. But I'm only on a month's trial, you know.
Alison:	You'll walk it. Won't she, Mrs. P?
Mrs. P.:	She's certainly above average.
Alison:	Us being average, eh Shelley?
Shelley	(*preoccupied with work*): That's us.
Alison:	I'll have to be careful or they'll give you a job and sack me.
Shelley:	That might be less funny than you think.
Alison:	What d'you mean?
Shelley:	Jobs are going to be very tight around here.
Alison:	Still, that won't affect Clare, will it?
Shelley:	Can't tell. I hope not.
Mrs. P.:	So do I, dear. I shouldn't tell you things, Alison, but Mr. Neale asked me for a report on your progress, and I told him I'd be very happy to recommend you.
Alison:	Oh that's great, Mrs. P.
	(*Phone rings, which Mrs. P. answers.*)
Mrs. P.:	Yes. Well, there you are, Clare. Mr. Neale wants to see you in his office.
Clare:	Me? Now?
Mrs. P.:	Yes, off you go. I do hope it's good news.
Alison:	Good luck, Clare.
Shelley:	Good luck.
Clare:	Thanks. You've all been really nice to me. I hope . . . well, I hope I can stay.
	(She goes out. During the conversation that follows Mr. Neale's office should be lit, and Clare visible in it talking to Mr. Neale – although the audience hears nothing of their conversation.)
Shelley:	So do I, but I wouldn't bank on it.
Alison:	Why not? – she's very good.
Mrs. P.:	She can at least spell and punctuate.
Shelley:	It's not her that's the problem. Morley's going on

74

	about surplus staffing – he thinks there's millions of pounds to be made from cutting jobs.
Mrs. P.:	But Mr. Neale told her that if she did well she'd be taken on.
Shelley:	Taken in, more like.
Alison:	That's not fair, Shelley. He's dead nice, is Mr. Neale.
Shelley:	Oh, he's nice enough, but that's not the point. Neale's not in charge, is he? And if Morley says there's no job, then there's no job.
Mrs. P.:	Well, that wouldn't be fair.
Shelley:	No, Mrs. P., it wouldn't, but it still might happen.
Alison:	Well, I just hope she gets the job, that's all.
Mrs. P.:	I do hope so, for her sake.

(Clare returns, obviously a bit upset.)

Alison:	They're not going to let you stay, are they?
Clare:	No.
Alison:	I'm sorry. We all are.
Shelley:	Yeah.
Mrs. P.:	Well, I must say I thought better of Mr. Neale.
Clare:	Oh no, he was ever so nice. I think he was sorry, he seemed a bit embarrassed.
Alison:	It doesn't help you, though, does it?
Clare:	But it's not up to him. They've just had some rule from head office that stops them taking on new staff.
Alison:	Just like that, with no warning. It's ridiculous.
Mrs. P.:	Well, Shelley, what's your precious union going to do about it?
Clare:	No, please don't make a fuss.
Shelley:	There's not much we can do.
Mrs. P.:	Huh. Typical.
Shelley:	Come off it, Mrs. P. Clare's not a full member, she's not paid a sub, –
Alison:	How d'you expect her to, she's only on a month's trial?
Shelley:	I know that. I'm not blaming her. I'm just saying that there's not much the union can do, if she's not a full member and there's been no breach of contract.
Mrs. P.:	Mr. Neale promised her a job if she worked well, and no one can say she hasn't worked well.
Clare:	Please, it's very kind of you, but I'd rather there wasn't any trouble.
Shelley:	No, fair enough. I'll see him. I'm not hopeful, but it's worth a try. Besides, I can't have Mrs. P. thinking I'm not militant enough. *(Goes cheerily out.)*
Alison:	Shelley the human time bomb, going off again.
Mrs. P.:	Well I'd far rather she did something for a girl like Clare than spend all her energy on those silly meetings, or haggling over money.

Clare:	It's nice of you to bother, but I really don't think it'll make any difference.
Alison:	What did he say?
Clare:	Well, he did say he was very pleased with how I'd done, and said Mrs. P. had given me a good report and normally he'd be very happy to offer me a job.
Mrs. P.:	He's out of his senses, turning away a girl like you.
Clare:	But he said he'd just had this new rule, and there was no way round it.
Alison:	Did he say there might be a chance later on?
Clare:	Well, I think there might be, but I'm not sure. To be honest, I don't think he knows what's going to happen.

(C) Mr. Neale's office. Shelley enters, almost without knocking.

Shelley:	Mr. Neale?
Neale:	Oh, hello Shelley. Sit down.
Shelley:	What's this about Clare not being taken on?
Neale:	That's just it. She's not being taken on. She can't be.
Shelley:	But you told her, in the office, that if she made a good start . . .
Neale:	Yes, I know . . .
Shelley:	If she made a good start, she'd have a job. 'See how you go,' you said. And now she's going – out.
Neale:	Shelley, believe me, I couldn't know about the freeze.
Shelley:	Well, why not keep to your word, then? I mean, it is a kind of agreement, isn't it, Mr. Neale?
Neale:	Now then, don't threaten me. You couldn't hold me to it. They wouldn't let you.
Shelley:	No?
Neale:	No. You might get me sacked but you wouldn't get Clare a job. I tried, honestly I did, but there's no chance. Head office would refuse to take her – or anyone else.
Shelley:	For ever?
Neale:	Oh no. Just a short-term freeze.
Shelley:	Till when?
Neale:	I don't know. They didn't tell me.
Shelley:	Or anyone else.
Neale:	I'm afraid not.
Shelley:	But that's a crazy way to run a firm. (*Pause.*) I said, that's a crazy way to run a firm.
Neale:	You don't expect me to comment on that, do you?
Shelley:	You don't need to. But you must agree, it's a daft way to do business. You should never have taken her on in the first place, if there wasn't a job to give her.

Neale:	Of course not, but how could I know?
Shelley:	They should tell you.
Neale:	Well, maybe, but –
Shelley:	But you can't tell them, right? Well we can. I'll get back to union headquarters, but your head office might just be hearing from us. Good bye, Mr. Neale.
Neale:	Good bye, Shelley. Oh – and thank you. I am sorry about Clare, truly.
Shelley:	Yes, I know. You're like me – a softy at heart. (*Goes out.*)

(D) The typists' office.

Alison:	You'll stay till the end of the month, then?
Clare:	Oh yes. Besides, I've nothing else.
Alison:	It's not easy, is it? And you might have got something else while you were here, if only you'd known.
Clare:	You can't tell. Never mind, a month's work is better than none, I suppose.
Mrs. P.:	Well, I think it's shocking.
Shelley	(*entering*): Quite agree, Mrs. P., but we can't beat it.
Alison:	Never mind, Shelley, you can't win 'em all.
Mrs. P.:	So the mighty union can't help a girl from losing her job.
Shelley:	It's not her job, Mrs. P., it's theirs – and they're freezing it. No, I'm sorry, Clare, I don't think there's much we can do this time.
Mrs. P.:	What d'you mean, this time? She's leaving.
Shelley:	There'll be a next time for somebody, maybe not Clare. And next time we can make them think before they take people on trial.
Alison:	But that doesn't help Clare, does it?
Clare:	No, but it will help someone else.
Shelley:	Right, and that's worth it, eh?
Clare:	Yes, Shelley, it is. Thanks for trying, anyway.
Mrs. P.:	Well, girls, it's two minutes to five o'clock. I suggest you stop pretending you're doing any work and we'll finish early. All right?
Alison:	Quick, before she changes her mind.
Shelley:	Mrs. P., I think you're coming round. We'll make a militant of you yet.
Mrs. P.:	Never.

A Sense of Purpose

Adi, *a young man*
Johanna, *his aunt*
Herr Roller, *a stage*
    designer

Kurt
Helga } *students*
Magda
Kubizek, *Adi's friend*

The play takes place in Vienna, early in this century.

Scene One

Aunt Johanna and her nephew Adi, waiting in a sitting-room for Herr Roller to arrive.

Aunt: Now, dear, are you sure you want to see Herr Roller?

Adi: Of course, Aunt Johanna. I am most extremely grateful for all . . .

Aunt: It's all right. You needn't bother with all that. But you know the theatre isn't an easy life.

Adi: I don't want an easy life. I want to do something that's worthwhile. Opera is the finest thing I know, and Herr Roller is the best stage designer in Vienna. I want to work with him.

Aunt: Very well, but it may be hard.

Adi: I'm prepared for that.

Aunt: I know you've been on your own since your mother's death . . .

Adi: Not alone, Aunt Johanna. Don't forget Kubizek.

Aunt: Having the company of a young man your own age is not the same as having a parent to guide you. Vienna's a dangerous place for a boy of eighteen.

Adi: I'll be all right.

Aunt: Well, at least you'll be all right for money. There's your father's inheritance, and your mother left you a good ninety crowns a month, so you shouldn't starve. And I'll make sure you get a bit extra.

Adi:	We'll be all right, aunt, don't you worry.
Aunt:	But you will keep up your studies?
Adi:	Oh yes. Kubizek goes to music college, and I have my painting.
Aunt:	I know, dear, but it's not good for you to work on your own. You ought to go to the Academy.
Adi:	I will do. I'm just waiting for them to accept me.
Aunt:	My word, you are confident. I'm sure you'll make a name for yourself. Here's Herr Roller now. *(Herr Roller enters, and goes to her.)*
Roller:	Ah, Frau Gellner.
Aunt:	Herr Roller, how good of you to come.
Roller:	And this is your nephew Adi?
Adi:	I'm most honoured to greet you, Herr Roller.
Aunt:	I'll leave you to your discussions, then. Goodbye, Herr Roller. Goodbye, Adi, and good luck. *(He bows, as she goes out.)*
Roller:	Right. Sit down, young man. *(Both sit.)* So, you want to design sets for the opera?
Adi:	More than anything else in the world.
Roller:	It's not easy.
Adi:	I don't want to do anything that is easy.
Roller:	There's a lot of competition . . .
Adi:	I am not afraid to put my ideas before the world.
Roller:	I see. You . . . er . . . might need to start in a rather modest way . . .
Adi:	I don't understand.
Roller:	Well, let's see. You don't have any training, do you? An Academy course?
Adi:	I have applied. I passed the entrance examination . . .
Roller:	Ah yes, the initial test. Have they accepted your folio?
Adi:	They have my paintings at the moment. I expect to hear of their acceptance very soon.
Roller:	Even so, it will take time. You will need a period of training and then some years as an assistant before you can hope to design your own sets.
Adi:	But I can hope?
Roller:	Oh yes, indeed. Anyone can hope. You like opera?
Adi:	Opera, Herr Roller, is the passion of my life. Wagner is the finest genius Germany has produced.
Roller:	Wagner? I should have thought a young man like you would prefer more modern music. Berg, perhaps?
Adi:	Never. No one but Wagner.
Roller:	I see. You seem very sure of your ground.
Adi:	I am. Thank you, Herr Roller, for your assistance. *(Rises.)*

Roller: You're welcome, young man. I'm always pleased to be of use to Frau Gellner. Let me know when you finish your course. Good day. (*They shake hands, and leave.*)

Scene Two

Kurt, Helga and Magda seated round a table in a cafe, looking through examination lists, talking excitedly and laughing. Kurt sees Adi approaching.

Kurt: Sssh. Put it away. Don't talk about them.

Adi (*approaching but not sitting down*): You have the results?

Kurt: Er . . . yes . . . er, yes, I think the Art results are here. (*He hands them over. Adi goes through the lists, looking for his name without success. Kurt hands him an envelope.*) And they gave me this to give to you.

Adi (*taking the envelope without saying anything. He opens it and reads quickly. Throughout the scene he remains standing*): The fools! Idiots! They must be blind.

Kurt: Bad luck. They've been very strict this year.

Adi: Strict? Strict? They've not been strict – they've been stupid. Pathetic pipsqueaks . . . what do they know about art?

Helga: Quite a lot if they're running the Academy.

Adi: They know a lot about the past. They know the old art, the safe things. They couldn't tell real, new art if it was staring them in the face.

Magda: What does it say?

Adi: Mmm? Oh . . . 'Dear Sir, we regret to inform you . . .' blah, blah, blah . . . '. . . we respectfully suggest that you apply to study architecture in the next academic year.'

Magda: Don't you think that would be a good idea?

Helga: Not if you're going to earn any money – it'd be another year before you start college.

Adi: There are more important things than money.

Kurt: And even then you'd have to pass the exams. You'd have to go back to school.

Adi: It's out of the question. I wouldn't go back to those idiots for anything.

Magda: But if it would help?

Adi: Help? Teachers? How can teachers help anything? They're a collection of moth-eaten fatheads without a single original idea between them. If they could do

	something, they'd do it; but they can't, so they teach. What did teachers ever do for Wagner? They thought Wagner was stupid – that's how clever teachers are.
Kurt:	But you do need the exams.
Adi:	Exams? Tests? Teaching you to jump through hoops? Fussing about spelling and punctuation when what matters is ideas.
Kurt:	How d'you mean?
Adi:	How many teachers do you know who could write an opera? Heh?
Magda:	Have you written one, then?
Adi:	Well, it's not finished yet, but it will be. It's from an idea of Wagner's.
Magda:	You're keen on opera, then?
Helga:	Interested in the girls outside, more like.
Adi:	They're foul, obscene. An insult to Vienna.
Helga	(*with a knowing smile*): That's not what I heard.
Magda	(*embarrassed*): But you do write music?
Adi:	A little. Kubizek, my collaborator, helps me some of the time.
Kurt:	Kubizek, I've seen him around. Doesn't he go to Parliament?
Adi:	We go together. We're students of politics.
Helga:	What on earth d'you go to Parliament for?
Kurt:	It's important.
Helga:	Huh. It's certainly boring. A whole lot of middle-aged men yelling at each other and getting nowhere. It's not my idea of fun.
Kurt:	It's not meant to be fun.
Magda:	But surely there's no reason why people shouldn't go if they want.
Kurt:	People should go. They should be made to . . .
Adi	(*a sudden, powerful interruption*): It's disgusting. It's a bitter, disorganised shambles, and for most of the time they don't even speak in our own language.
Kurt:	But if that's how you feel . . .
Adi	(*ignoring him*): But it is important. That's where things can be decided. At present, it's of no use. But in the future, it could be used.
Kurt:	For the people, you mean? The workers.
Magda:	You're not a communist, are you?
Adi:	Never. Don't talk to me about the workers.
Helga:	Too good for them, are you?
Adi:	I've seen them. I've worked with them.
Kurt:	Where?
Adi:	On a building site last summer. They stopped me. The workers stopped me – stopped me working.

Magda:	For no reason?
Adi:	They said it was because I wouldn't join a union, but –
Kurt:	Oh well. You can't blame them.
Adi:	Who can't blame them? Of course I blame them.
Magda:	But why did they . . .
Adi:	Don't ask me. I don't understand. Just don't try to tell me about the workers, that's all.
Helga	(*nastily*): You've not heard from the army yet, then?
Adi	(*suddenly restless*): Er . . . I'm sorry, I must get back. (*Moves away.*)
Magda:	Must you?
Adi:	Yes. Goodbye. (*He bows rather stiffly, and goes out.*)
Helga:	Well, he's a little charmer all right, isn't he?
Magda:	I think he's just a bit shy.
Helga:	Shy? He's got the biggest head I've ever seen.
Kurt:	Perhaps that's why he doesn't want to be called up.
Magda:	How d'you mean?
Kurt:	Perhaps he's scared the army will tell him what to do, push him around a bit. He likes to be his own boss.
Magda:	It isn't just that.
Helga:	What do you know about it?
Magda:	I heard him talking about it last week.
Helga:	And what did he say?
Magda:	He said he couldn't see the point of marching up and down for a rotten government when there wasn't a war on and he'd got work to do.
Helga:	Work? The only work he does is chatting up the tarts outside the opera.
Magda:	I don't believe that.
Helga:	All right, don't. But that's what they say.
Kurt:	Come on, then, tell us. What work does he do?
Magda:	Don't ask me, I hardly know him. But it's obviously important.
Kurt:	Important to him. I'm not sure about the rest of us.
Magda:	But at least he's trying.
Helga:	Trying? He's more than trying – he's exhausting.
Magda:	Can't you ever be serious? Can't you see that he doesn't just accept things as they are, do what everyone else does. He's looking . . .
Kurt:	Yes, but what for? Looking for what?
Magda:	I don't know. Something else.

Scene Three

A simple room in a men's hostel. Kubizek enters, puts down a few paintings and sits down to count the money he's collected. Adi comes in.

Kubizek: Not a bad haul. Twenty-five crowns this week.
Adi: Mmm?
Kubizek: You're not a genius, but you sell some paintings.
Adi: Don't talk to me about paintings.
Kubizek: Why not? They make money, don't they?
Adi: Don't talk about them.
Kubizek: All right. (*An uneasy pause*) Did you hear from the Academy?
Adi: I've been thinking about architecture.
Kubizek: Do they do that as well?
Adi: Architecture affects people; paintings just sit in galleries, but people live in buildings. I've been thinking about Linz, where I used to live. I could rebuild Linz, design it the way it really ought to be . . .
Kubizek: Will they let you do that?
Adi: Who?
Kubizek: The Academy.
Adi: Who cares about the Academy? A bunch of second-rate minds buried in the past. They can't see what's happening.
Kubizek: Aren't you going to go, then?
Adi: I must stay free. I can't do good work if I'm tied down to petty courses, attending lectures, sitting exams. That's not what my life's about. There's work to be done.
Kubizek: Don't tell me. I've three compositions to finish by Friday.
Adi: Not that work. The real work. Our country's work.
Kubizek: What's that, then?
Adi: Look around you. Look at the businesses, the little corner shops closing down, the newspapers, . . .
Kubizek: Yes?
Adi: Who's doing well, who's doing badly?
Kubizek: Well, we're managing.
Adi: We're managing, but only just. Who's really managing, eh? I'll tell you. Foreigners. They're managing, managing quite nicely, thank you very much. They're managing the shops that are making a profit, they're managing the banks, and the press, and –

Kubizek:	Well, we can't all be millionaires.
Adi:	While they're around, none of *us* can be anything.
Kubizek:	Well, they've got to live, haven't they? And if you stop doing paintings, what are we going to live on?
Adi:	I'll starve if need be. I'll dedicate myself.
Kubizek:	What to, opera? It's a neat idea, I know, but –
Adi:	I'm not talking about opera. That's over.
Kubizek:	But you haven't finished it yet. Nothing like.
Adi:	It's over.
Kubizek:	You mean you're giving up, just like that?
Adi:	There are more important things.
Kubizek:	That's what I told you at two in the morning when you wanted some harmonies, but it didn't stop you waking me up.
Adi:	That was just a dream. I was a child. Now, there is men's work to be done. Politics.
Kubizek:	Oh no, you're not standing for Parliament?
Adi:	Not yet.
Kubizek:	But you saw them. Middle-aged fools, talking another language.
Adi:	Exactly. Another language . . . nothing to care about, nothing to fight for, nothing to fight against. Our people have no reason to care. We must give them a cause to fight for, something to love.
	(*Magda enters, timidly.*)
Magda:	I'm sorry. Am I interrupting?
Kubizek:	Oh no, not at all, I was just going out for some cigarettes.
Adi:	No, Kubizek, stay. This is important.
Kubizek:	Later. We'll talk about it later. (*To Magda*) Nice to meet you. (*He goes out, leaving Magda and Adi very uneasy.*)
Magda:	Hello. I hope you don't mind.
Adi:	No. Er . . .
Magda:	I'm sorry. I just thought . . . you're not angry, are you?
Adi:	Angry?
Magda:	I wanted to see you. I told Helga it's just that you're shy –
Adi:	What?
Magda:	She said that . . . you, know, about the girls at the opera . . .
Adi:	They're disgusting. A curse to our country.
Magda:	Of course, yes. I mean, she was only joking. (*Pause.*) I was interested. In what you were saying this morning. I think you've got some good ideas.
Adi:	I've got work to do, I'm sorry.
Magda:	Oh, really? What are you working on?

Adi   (*almost to himself*): I've got to work – in Germany. That's where I must be, where my future lies. I can't stay in Vienna . . .

Magda: Shall I come back later?

Adi   (*starts packing a case, furiously*): Tell Kubizek that I'm going – to Munich. It's complicated – but I've got to go. I was trying to explain. Look, we need, *we* need, the country needs, to know what we're doing, where we're going, who we are. How can we care about ourselves if we're all mixed up, pushed around by foreigners? I mean, –

Magda: Look, if I shouldn't have come –

Adi: Goodbye. (*He goes out, abruptly, leaving Magda standing surprised. After a moment Kubizek enters.*)

Kubizek: Oh, sorry. I thought you must have gone. I heard the door.

Magda: No. He's gone.

Kubizek: But he's only just come in.

Magda: No, he's gone away. For good.

Kubizek: Are you serious?

Magda: Yes. He's left. Said he was going to Munich. Tell me, is it true he's trying to get out of being called up for the army?

Kubizek: Mmm. Well, that's part of it, but it's not that simple. He's no coward. I mean, if there was a war on he'd be there in no time. It's complicated . . .

Magda: That's what he said.

Kubizek: Yes. Well, he's right.

Magda: Still, he's interesting – a bit different. Do you think he'd mind if I wrote to him?

Kubizek: He might. I don't know, I don't really understand him. Mind you, things'll be a lot duller if he has gone. Where will you write to?

Magda: I don't know. (*Looks round the room*) Somewhere like this, I suppose. Men's hostel, that sort of thing.

Kubizek: Well, you can try.

Magda: I've just realised, I only know him as Adi. What's his proper name?

Kubizek: That's easy. Adolf – Adolf Hitler.

Assignments

Play-Reading and Performance

This collection of plays is intended for reading and study in class, and also for performance. However, only the Slaney home in *Changes in the Air* would really justify the work and expense involved in providing a detailed setting; generally, the plays work best in simple settings which allow the smoothest possible movement between scenes.

Songs

All the lyrics included in this collection have been set to music for performance, but there is a strong case for making such presentations as 'home-grown' as possible. I would therefore strongly encourage teachers and pupils involved in performing any of these plays to write their own music, and I hope they enjoy the result as much as we did.

Assignments

A word of warning – for teachers.
The assignments which follow involve very different kinds of thinking and need to be read before being set. Some might benefit from interdepartmental collaboration, while others will involve some basic research and quite a lot of working time. They are, of course, only suggested models, and it is hoped that teachers will build on and adapt the suggestions offered here to suit the needs of their pupils.

A Whole Lot of Grief

This play was written for a group of boys in their last year at school. Many of them had not read any plays which interested them, but they were attracted by the idea of a play about a gangster, and their performance of it as a lunchtime entertainment was very successful.

The play is not just Al Capone in action; it looks at the people in the story as well as at what happens. To write it I read a biography of Al Capone, and a book partly written by Eliot Ness. These gave me the main events of the action (Ness' interview, the killing of Basile, the final procession), but also a lot of useful details – Mrs. Freeman's operations, the newsboy, Tony the Greek, the method of killing O'Banion and so on.

Comprehension

1 Scene 1: make two columns, headed FOR and AGAINST, and put each of the characters in this scene in one of the columns. Then explain why you think this scene is included; what does it add to the story?

2 Scene 5: read through the scene carefully, and then draw a diagram of the positions of O'Banion, Fred, Lombardo and the Kid at the time of the shooting. (Rehearse it in a group if possible.)

Underneath your diagram, write your reasons for putting people where you have put them, and explain (a) why O'Banion was killed; (b) the difference in reaction between Lombardo and the Kid.

Character

1 What do we learn about the gangster world from Tony the Greek, Basile and the Kid? (Scenes 2–5)

2 Look carefully at the behaviour of the Capone gang in scenes 7 and 9. Describe each member as fully as you can (apart from Al Capone), and say what you think would have happened after Capone's arrest.

Possible questions: Who is strongest?
Who is weakest?
Is the gang divided in any way? How? Why?
Would they wait for Capone to come back from prison?

Main Characters

1 Write a character study of Eliot Ness, trying to find words that describe the sort of person he is. Back up what you say with quotations from the play, like these examples:

'Oh yes, we'd break him.' (p. 7, Scene 4)

'A lot of guys seem to want a kick in the seat, and we might make sure they get it.' (p. 11, Scene 6)

'It just means we're going to have to be that bit better, that's all.' (p. 13, Scene 8)

Each of these show a different part of Ness' character. Work out what they tell you about him, and then find quotations of your own.

2 Write a character study of Al Capone, covering the different sides of his

character and describing how he changes as the play goes on. Find at least four separate quotations to back up what you say (like those for Eliot Ness above), and choose words which describe his personality. Some of these may help:

kind   cruel   angry   mad   clever   wise   stupid   tough   wicked
lonely   sad   confident   proud   shy   frightened   frightening

3 'I'd rather go for Scarface than Ness.' (p. 12, Scene 7)

Lombardo compares Capone with Ness, and the play invites you to look at the two men together. Read through scenes 8 and 9, and then work out what Ness and Capone have in common, and how they are different. Why are they never on stage together?

The Song

There are three verses to the song, one at the beginning, one in the middle and one at the end. Is there any reason why the second verse comes after Scene Five?

The song does not tell a story, but it picks out some of the feelings that are already there. Describe the different feelings in each verse, and say as much as you can about the way the last four lines change. (What stays the same? What changes? Why? What did you think of it?)

Writing

1 Write your own scene, about

Either   (a) Eliot Ness and his wife
Or   (b) Al Capone in prison

2 This play gives a portrait of Al Capone by showing you different views. You see Al relaxing with someone he can trust (Tony the Greek, in Scene 2), and you hear about him from policemen who want to arrest him (Scene 4). Write your own play scenes – at least two – in which you deal with one of the following characters from two different points of view:

Robin Hood   Joan of Arc   Queen Elizabeth I
Oliver Cromwell   Mrs. Pankhurst   Winston Churchill

3 Alternate Scenes: The play moves mainly between two areas (the gang and the police), so that the scenes alternate gang:police:gang. This way of writing is sometimes called *cinematic*, because it moves quickly from one scene to another, like many films. It is not new, however. Shakespeare used it a lot in his Roman plays and History plays.

Plan your own outline for a play which tells the story of a clash between two sides. Build up the action one step at a time; write about five lines on each scene.

Possible subjects:
  The Gunpowder plot (conspirators/government spies)
  Charge of the Light Brigade (British/Russians)
  Little Big Horn (Custer and officers/Sitting Bull)
  El Alamein (Montgomery/Rommel)

Improvisation

1 Using Dave's account (p. 10, Scene 6) and any other information you can find, act out the St. Valentine's Day Massacre.
2 Turn your working group into a gang, and work out one or more of the following scenes:
  a new member joining
  choosing a leader
  preparing for a fight
  reactions when something goes wrong
  interrogation by the police

Assassination

This play was written at a time when there were many demonstrations by students all over the world, protesting against their governments. Because England is fairly peaceful, we tend to forget that power can change hands suddenly and violently. Durium is an imaginary country which is small, underdeveloped and easily affected by what happens to its ruler.

Setting

Assassination takes place in Europe, but not in England.
(a) How is this made clear to the audience?
(b) How would the play be different if it was set in England?

Acting

What problems does Scene Two present for actors? Imagine that you are directing the play, and write your notes for this scene. What will you do about:
  characters and voices
  seating
  movements
  key moments
  furniture, props and costumes.

Comprehension

Scene 1: Marianne, the Premier's daughter, is talking with Marc and Petra.
1 Why does Marc criticise Heller?
2 What does Petra think of (a) Heller (b) Marc?
3 Which two things are due to happen at the Hellers'?

Scene 2: 1 The committee decides –
(a) to murder Heller
(b) to organise a march
(c) to kill Molluk
2 According to Carlo, what could be worse than Heller?
(a) his daughter
(b) the government
(c) Molluk
3 Who is sure that Molluk's taken care of?
(a) Jerome
(b) Viktor
(c) Kristina
4 Andrei is
(a) eager for action
(b) worried about the murder
(c) careful over details
5 Marc is told
(a) nothing
(b) a lie
(c) the whole plot

Scene 3: How does Molluk get rid of Korpov?
        Why does he want to get rid of him?
Scene 4: Why is Marianne bitter?
        How well does Marc know Andrei?
Scene 5: Why are the committee worried?
        Who is most likely to have told the police about Andrei?
Scene 6: How do you know Molluk was expecting to take over?
        Could Heller have been saved? How?

Characters and Ideas

1 Describe briefly (5 lines each) the way each of the following people think about politics:

Petra   Carlo   Jerome   Mrs. Heller

2 In what ways are Heller and Molluk different
(a) as people?
(b) as politicians?
Use quotations from the play to back up your points; look for things that they do and say, and for things that other people say about them.

Writing

1 Write a scene which takes place after the ending of this play,
including *either* (a) Mrs. Heller, Marianne and Marc
      or   (b) Viktor, Alex and Carlo.
You may use other characters apart from these, but try to make any characters
that you do use the same sort of people that they are in the play.

2 Look back through the play, especially Scene 6, and notice how it speeds up at
the end – a lot of short scenes, moving towards the climax of the assassination.
Write your own political play, also set in an imaginary country of your own,
which builds up to a climax at the end. Possible events:

> a politician resigning
> the result of an election
> a new act of Parliament is passed
> war is declared.

Improvisation

1 A group of conspirators are talking about planting a bomb. They all agree on
the cause for which they are working, but they differ in their feelings about the
bomb and its impact on other people.

2 A group of conspirators suspect that one of them is a traitor, but they do not
know who. There are no easy clues, or messages from outside; no one leaves,
or comes in. The group, as a group, try to find out who has betrayed them.

3 To the people of Durium, the play's final announcement will come as a shock.
In groups, work out different ways in which the news might affect various
groups of people who hear the radio message.

Changes in the Air

Changes in the Air was first performed in Belper in 1977, two hundred years after
Jedediah Strutt built his first mill in Belper. It was a local play, and it borrowed a
lot from an excellent history book by a local man – E. G. Power's *A Textile
Community in the Industrial Revolution*.

Oliver the Spy and Robert Blincowe both come straight from real life, and a
lot of the details are also real – there was a Bill Blount who dug up the roads for
coal, there was a violent football match at Duffield and so on. On the other
hand, the play squeezes the events of forty years into two hours, and in writing
it I made some things up and joined others together which actually happened
separately.

The play is not just a story about the past. It looks at complicated ideas like
freedom and order, rebellion and peace, progress and change. It looks at them

from different points of view; there is not one story of the growth of the mills, there are several, and sometimes they disagree. That's why it may not be easy to say whether the play is for or against the changes that took place. A lot of the important thinking has to be done by the audience – or the reader.

Structure

Copy out the grid given below:

	1	2	3	4	5	6	7	8	9	10	11
Slaney family											
Strutt mill											
Pentrich revolt											

Place a tick under each scene number, opposite the heading which you think fits that scene best. In some cases you may want to put two ticks for one scene. If you can think of other important headings which need to be added, put them in and tick the scenes where they appear.

When you've been through the whole play, try to work out which of the following describes the play best:

Changes in the Air is about: (a) mill-workers
(b) the end of the nailers
(c) a family
(d) the need to defend yourself
(e) progress
(f) rebels
(g) how to behave
(h) George Strutt

Arrange these in order of preference, and then write your own sentence which begins Changes in the Air is about – . . .

Questions

1 What signs are there in Scenes 2 and 3 that the Slaneys suffer because of their lack of education?

2 In performance, there would probably need to be an interval. Should it be between Scenes 4 and 5, or between Scenes 5 and 6? Explain the reasons for your choice as fully as possible.

3 In Scene 5, how does the incident of the Parkin boy show us the differences between Oliver and the others?

Characters

1 Many of the characters (Oliver, Robert Blincowe, Rev. Isaac Ludlam) were real people. The whole Slaney family, however, were made up. Describe them, and try to work out why they are the way they are; e.g. how they interact as people, why they are not all against the mill.

2 Describe John Watson and Richard Miller. Would the play be worse without them? Why/Why not? How do they differ from each other?

Gains and Losses

The play shows the impact of the mills upon a number of people, and their reactions vary a lot. In one sentence for each, sum up the feelings of the following about the changes that are taking place:

> Grandmother
> Will
> Robert Blincowe
> Rev. Ludlam
> Ephraim Ward
> George Strutt

The Songs

1 The ballad 'Changes in the Air' that goes right through the play is connected with the story of various scenes, but also expresses people's feelings about what is going on. Describe how these change through the play, and try to work out how you think the song should be performed on the stage. Who should sing it – a character, a separate singer, a group or a number of different singers? Where from – the centre of the stage, on the side, from offstage? What kind of accompaniment should there be?

2 Describe each of the other songs carefully, saying what sort of effect they ought to have on an audience (think about: music, backing, speed, voices, atmosphere, movement etc.).

Scene 1 – Saint Monday Song
Scene 3 – 'We are not Greek philosophers . . .'
Scene 8 – Ellen's song
Scene 9 – Revolution Song (words actually sung at the time)

Drama and Information

Look carefully at Scene 7.

This play is about things and ideas as well as people. That makes it more interesting, but also more dificult; it is easier to write and read about what Will did than to look at what his promotion means.

In Scene 7, very little happens except that we get the news of Will's marriage and promotion. On the other hand, the scene does put over some information that the audience needs, and gives different reactions to it:

(a) Which information in this scene is important?

(b) Richard Miller and John Watson disagree in their attitude to Will's cottage; who do you think is right, and why?

Writing Plays

1 Try to write a play scene which uses information but would also be interesting to watch. You will need to collect facts, and invent characters who are different from each other.

Possible subjects: disease in Elizabethan England
prison conditions
the railway navvies
the workhouse
Victorian schools

2 The play shows the impact of an event on a community of people. Work out your own play which deals with an important event or issue, which will affect different people in different ways.

Possible examples: the Civil War
the Plague
the Great Fire of London
invasion
the General Strike
the Blitz
a nuclear attack

Improvisation

1 Make up a scene – or group of scenes – about what happens to Simon Parkin's boy (Scene 5, p. 51).

2 In real life, Jeremiah Brandreth and Isaac Ludlam were hanged. Work on a scene involving *either* their trial *or* their cell in jail. Think about the differences between them.

3 Act out Robert Blincowe's return to Litton Mill.

4 Look at the mime in Scene 3 (pp. 46–7). Then work out your own work-mime on one of the following:

a slave galley
a car assembly line
a kitchen in a large, busy restaurant
putting up a marquee

Make up your own chant if you can, to go with the actions.

See How You Go

The Whole Play

Design a hand-out advertising a performance of this play. Make up all the necessary details (who's performing it, where and when) and write comments of your own that would sum up what it's about and make people want to see it. Maximum: 50 words.

Structure

This play is about something that happens in an office. Why do you think Scene 2 is included? What does it add to the play? Would the play be better or worse if it was left out? Explain your views as fully as you can.

Comprehension

Look at each of the following lines carefully, and for each one go back to the page it is on and remember what happens. Then, for each one, write what it is about and why it is important to the play.

Grandad: That's what we fought for, and it don't change (page 72).
Mrs. Holden: Huh. Workers of the world unite (page 72).
Shelley: Oh, he's nice enough, but that's not the point (page 75).
Clare: Yes, Shelley, it is (page 77).

Character

1 Read carefully through Scene 1(B). These are two of the things Mr. Neale says:

'I thought I ought to ask Miss Firth in, just to keep the union informed.' (page 66)
'Well . . . er . . . we've decided . . . I've called you in . . .' (page 67)
What do these tell you about the sort of man Neale is?

2 Find *three* quotations from this scene which tell you something about the character of Mr. Morley, and comment on them. (Try to make each quote show you something different.)

3 Shelley, Alison and Clare are all girls of roughly the same age with the same sort of job. Describe as fully as possible the ways in which they are different from each other.

Ideas and Attitudes

One of the things this play is concerned with is the way people think about trade unions. In one full sentence for each, describe the attitude to unions of *four* of the following:

Mrs. Prentiss   Shelley   Mr. Morley   Mrs. Holden   Mr. Holden

What is Clare's own attitude? Does it change at all?
(Look especially at Scene 1(A) and Scene 3(D).)

Acting

Look carefully through Scene 2 and imagine it being acted.

1 Why do you think the stage direction for Grandad's entrance says he 'should not act like a caricature'?

2 Imagine that you are the director of this play, and write clear instructions for the actors playing *Mick* and *one other part*. Write about the way they should talk, move, treat other characters, and pick out any important moments or problems they need to think about.

The Ending

Do any of these words describe the ending?

tragic   comic   sad   happy   true-to-life   unreal   anti-climax

Write about 50 words on what you thought of the ending, and how you think an audience would feel about it. Try to think up different ways of how you might end this play, and say whether they're better or worse. Why?

Writing

1 Write *either* a scene where Clare goes home to tell her family what has
             happened
      or   a future scene between Morley, Neale and Mrs. Prentiss.

2 This is a fairly realistic play about someone who has an unlucky start to her job. Write your own exaggerated, imaginary scene about someone starting a job, where things go *either* very badly *or* very well. (It can be as daft or unlikely as you like, but try to make it entertaining.)

Improvisation

1 Work in large groups (6–10), trying to agree on the details of a work situation where there is some tension between workers and management.

Think of: what does the firm do or make?
              what do the workers object to?
              what do they want?
              why don't the management agree?

Then divide into two smaller groups, one of the workers and one of managers. Work on and act out *three* scenes, one of workers, one of management and one where the two come together.
(Then you might do it again, with a different situation, changing the two groups round so that workers become managers and managers workers.)

2 In groups of 5 or less work on your own family scene about someone who loses a job. Think out carefully how each member of the family will react, and what it will mean to them.

A Sense of Purpose

This play grew out of some work I did with a history teacher, who was teaching a class about the rise of Hitler. He wanted to put across some of the personal facts about him as well as his political views and the historical events he helped to create.

Hitler

The word 'Hitler' does not appear in the play until the final line.

1 Why do you think this is? (What thoughts would go through the audience's minds through the play, and at the end?)

2 Where in the play could it have been more obvious that Adi is Hitler? What has been done to make it harder to find that out?

Character

1. Hitler is famous as a mass murderer, as a powerful popular leader, and as a fanatic who took his own ideas very seriously.

(a) What evidence in the play is there for each of these three ways of looking at him?

(b) What picture of him does the play give? What sort of person is he, and in what ways is he different from the famous Hitler?

(c) In some ways, Adi is not a consistent character – he changes his mind and he contradicts himself. Find as many examples of this as you can. (Clues: – money, painting, architecture . . .)

Other characters

This play uses a lot of true details from Hitler's early life – his love of opera, especially Wagner; the meeting his aunt arranged with Herr Roller; his friend Kubicek; his dealings with the Academy, and so on.

The three characters in Scene 2, however, are fictional. Describe each of them, and try to work out how they help to bring out Adi's character.

Politics

Helga thinks Parliament is 'a whole lot of middle-aged men yelling at each other and getting nowhere'. Kurt thinks 'it's important' (both in Scene 2, p. 81).

Describe Adi's view of Parliament, and his political ambitions, as fully as you can. Find at least three quotations from the play to back up what you say.

Writing

This play offers an unfamiliar look at a character most people have heard of. Write your own play scene which looks in an unexpected way at a famous person. Possible examples:

Alexander   Jesus   Shakespeare
Henry Ford   Charlie Chaplin   Stalin

Improvisation

1 Make up your own scenes in which Hitler is important but does not actually appear – e.g.
German officers planning to rebel
an English family listening to the news
Hitler's soldiers just before his defeat
a prisoner of war arguing with a guard

2 Invent a dictator, as powerful as Hitler but completely different from him. Make up scenes which show your leader's rise to power, and his effect on his followers.